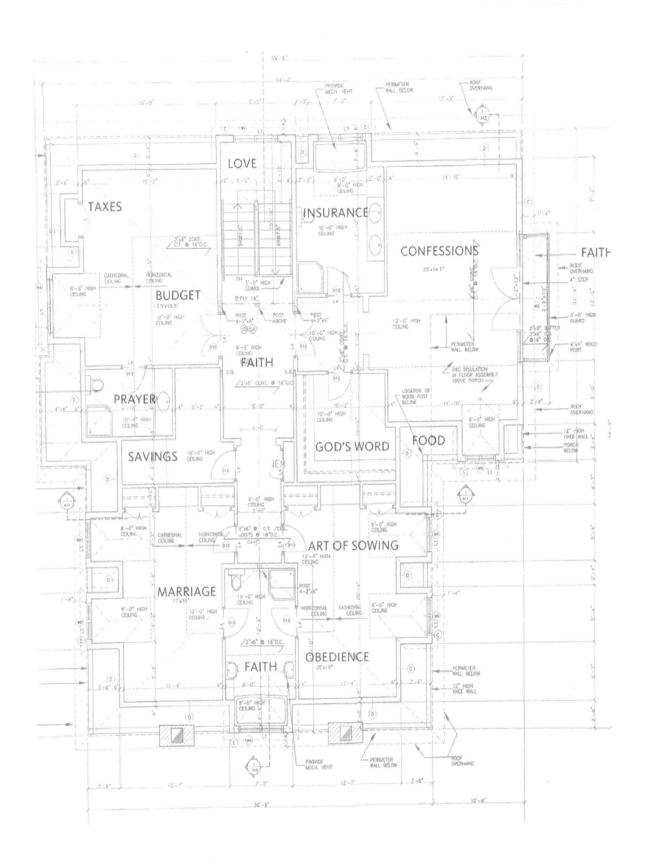

CUSTOM BUILT
A MARRIED COUPLE'S GUIDE TO BUILDING THEIR FINANCIAL HOME, *TOGETHER!*

For more information or to contact us, please visit www.crissevans.com

Acknowledgments

I would like to extend a heart of gratitude to my wonderful husband. I thank you for many years of supporting me in ministry, your heartfelt prayers and blessings over this project. Thank you for deciding thirteen years ago to take this journey with me to follow our Lord and Savior, Jesus Christ. Although we have experienced a lot of financial challenges, I'm grateful that we both stood rooted in God's Word as we defeated the enemy's attacks. We make a powerful team.

I would like to thank my amazing children, the three most important people in my life. I thank you for your love, support and sacrifices. I am forever thankful to God for blessing your dad and me with such great children. Continue to keep God first in your lives and walk fearlessly towards your purpose.

I would also like to thank my loving parents. Mom, you are such a great example of God's love. Thank you both for teaching others and me what God meant in His Word when He said, "...until death do you part." Happy 50th Anniversary!

Many thanks to my sister Candy for allowing God to use you to witness to me 13 years ago. Thank you for changing my family's life and mine forever.

Much love to my **S**isters **I**n **S**pirit (S.I.S) for your countless prayers and words of encouragement. You ladies are awesome!

My heartfelt expression of thanks also goes out to my Pastors, Dr. Creflo and Taffi Dollar, for your obedience in teaching the Word of God with simplicity and understanding. You have definitely made a mark in me that cannot be erased.

Very special thanks to four brilliant individuals: Pricilla Cheng, Brittany Brown, Cathy Upshire and Christopher Williams. Thank you for allowing God to use you and your talents for this project and helping me to equip the Body of Christ to be better stewards over their finances.

I cannot forget my Brothers and Sisters of the Personal Finance Support Ministry. I thank God for teaming me up with such a great group. It has been a privileged and an honor to serve alongside each of you. May God continue to bless you all!

TABLE OF CONTENTS

Introduction

Let me be the first to congratulate you on your decision to custom build your financial home God's way. As you diligently study God's Word and seek His promises regarding total life prosperity, I pray that you will confidently walk towards pursuing and achieving His best for your finances. The Word of God says in **Romans 11:36 (NLT)**

> *"For everything comes from Him and exists by His power and is intended for His glory."*

Meaning everything…yes everything; you, your spouse, your children, your house, your cars and even your money belong to God. He has appointed us as stewards over these things and trust that we will do what He instructs us to do with His stuff.

As we journey through this process of custom-building your financial home, I want you to think of me as your home inspector. As your inspector, I will follow you through each phase of the construction of your financial home and help you to identify code violations that are not in-line with God's Word. As you work to complete the plans that God has designed, I pray that you will discover new truths that will aid you in achieving your financial goals and visions together.

In Ephesians 1:18-19 (NCV), Paul best express my desire that I have for you as you complete this workbook…

> *"I pray also that you will have greater understanding in your heart so you will know the hope to which He has called us and that you will know how rich and glorious are the blessings God has promised His holy people. And you will know that God's power is very great for us who believe."*

CAUTION:

This book is not designed for you to just read; it is a tool that will aid you in implementing biblical principles in efforts of helping you to become a better steward over your finances.

There are six vital components to each phase:

Building Principles

At the beginning of each phase are biblical principles. They are fundamental truths that serve as a basis for establishing the foundation of your financial plans.

Memory Verses

This key verse of scripture will provide you with a word from God that support the over all principle of discussion for that phase.

Overviews

Each overview serves as an introduction to each phase, which provides you with an abstract of its content.

Questions

The questions serve as a means of testing your understanding of the principles discussed.

Building Blocks

The building blocks are additional scriptures located at the end of each phase and are in place to help guide and encourage you.

Say It & Create It

At the end of each phase is a confession (or space to fill in your own). This section was designed to help you practice using your mouth to speak life (not death) over your finances. The Word of God cautions us to be mindful of what we say, *"What you say can mean life or death. Those who speak with care will be rewarded"* **Proverbs 18:21 (NCV).** Therefore, this section provides you with words of life to speak over your finances.

~~~~~~

In Phase 7 you will find a **Certificate of Commitment**

This is a declaration that is designed to establish your commitment to each other towards becoming better stewards over the finances that God has blessed you with.

Pre-Financial Planning Check List

How much do you know about your finances?

	Yes	No	Unsure
-Do you know your fiancé/spouse's income?			
-Are you currently saving money?			
-Do you know your monthly household income?			
-Do you use a household budget each month?			
-Are you paying your bill on time each month?			
-Do you tithe?			
-Have you set financial goals as a couple?			
-Do you know your credit ratings?			
-Do you know how much debt you currently have?			
-Do you have sufficient insurance coverage?			
-Do you have medical coverage?			
-Do you have investments?			
-Are you currently working with a financial service professional?			
-Do you file tax returns annually? (joint if married)			
-Have you started preparing for retirement?			
-Have you prepared a will or trust?			

Let's inspect your old financial plans to avoid installing habits that will definitely not work in your new home.

Currently:	Needs Improvements	A Great Asset
Where are we in our...		
➢ Ability to discuss money	_____	_____
➢ Credit profile	_____	_____
➢ Knowledge of what God says about money	_____	_____
➢ Debt reduction plan	_____	_____
➢ Management of money	_____	_____
➢ Willingness to work as a team	_____	_____
➢ Retirement planning	_____	_____
➢ Ability to save	_____	_____
➢ Knowledge of investments	_____	_____
➢ Preparation of will(s) and/or trust(s)	_____	_____
➢ Purchase of life insurance	_____	_____
➢ Health insurance needs	_____	_____
➢ Organization of financial documents	_____	_____
➢ Giving of tithes & offerings	_____	_____
➢ Process of educating our children on good money management habits	_____	_____
➢ God's involvement in our finances	_____	_____

HIS

Let's inspect your old financial plans to avoid installing habits that will definitely not work in your new financial home.

Currently:	Needs Improvements	A Great Asset
Where are we in our...		
➤ Ability to discuss money	_____	_____
➤ Credit profile	_____	_____
➤ Knowledge of what God says about money	_____	_____
➤ Debt reduction plan	_____	_____
➤ Management of money	_____	_____
➤ Willingness to work as a team	_____	_____
➤ Retirement planning	_____	_____
➤ Ability to save	_____	_____
➤ Knowledge of investments	_____	_____
➤ Preparation of will(s) and/or trust(s)	_____	_____
➤ Purchase of life insurance	_____	_____
➤ Health insurance needs	_____	_____
➤ Organization of financial documents	_____	_____
➤ Giving of tithes & offerings	_____	_____
➤ Process of educating our children on good money management habits	_____	_____
➤ God's involvement in our finances	_____	_____

HERS

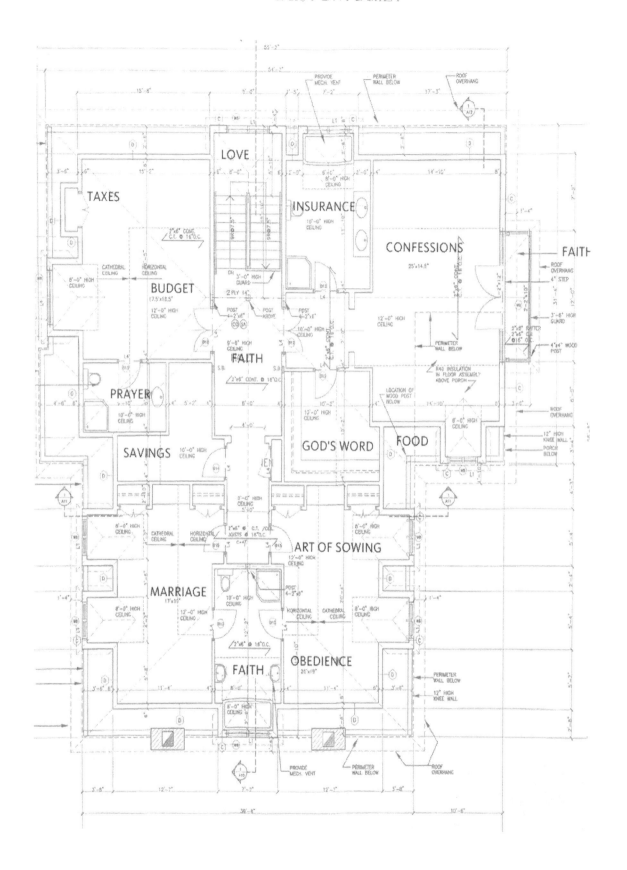

PHASE 1

Choosing Your Work-Crew

Phase 1

Choosing Your Work-Crew

Building Principle:

Couples are more successful when they work together.

Memory Verse:

"Two people are better off than one, for they can help each other succeed. If one person falls, the other can reach out and help. But someone who falls alone is in real trouble." **Ecclesiastes 4:9-10 (NLT)**

Overview

Building a physical home with just one person can be quite a challenge. Never have I seen a one-man team working to complete the construction of a new home. Whether you are married or engaged, you have already chosen one of your crew members to work with (your spouse/fiancé). God chose both of you. It is vital that you fully understand God's true purpose for your marriage, how your marriage fits into His plans, but most importantly, why we need Him in our plans.

Building Objectives

- ➤ Understand God's purpose for the institution of marriage.
- ➤ Encourage love and teamwork.
- ➤ Recognize the importance of God in your plan.
- ➤ Help you to see why Satan is not part of God's plan for your marriage.

God's Purpose For Your Marriage

The discussion of money within the confinements of marriage can be a topic of anxiety and discord. Due to the sensitivity of the topic you find couples approaching their financial discussions yelling and screaming or simply avoiding the topic altogether. It is not a secret that financial matters are major stressors within a marriage, which often leads to separation and eventually divorce. The real secret is that it doesn't have to be that way. It's sad that even today, every other marriage statistically ends in divorce, and that there are no statistical differences among married believers.

I too have experienced years of tiptoeing around the subject of money within my own marriage. I've tried to disguise the topic by changing the title of a budget form to a "*family expense plan*", and even gone on financial date nights and financial planning weekend getaways. No matter how much I tried to dress it up, the subject appeared to be a topic of tension. It was not until I decided to turn my cares over to God in prayer that we both were loosed from the strongholds of our finances. God gave me wisdom on what to say, how to say it and the proper time to say it. On the other hand, God prepared my husband's heart to receive His truths regarding stewardship.

God has great plans for your lives together; the key is working the plans *together*.

Satan on the other hand has his great plans of financial dysfunction sketched out for your marriage and it involves lack of financial harmony. Satan can keep you in total disagreement and unable to communicate about money, thereby ruining your home financially. He will leave you with an abandoned building full of lost dreams and aspirations, lost hopes and bad memories, instead of the dream that God purposed in His plan when He initially put you together. The enemy has been clever in recognizing that the same tactics that he has successfully used in the marriages of non-believers are also effective in destroying believers' marriages. Satan knows the great potential of God's design for your marriage and that's why he diligently entices couples to follow his plans.

Recognize God's authority in your marriage and *together* make a true commitment to follow His plans for the marriage that you desire and that He designed.

> "*For we are God's [own] handiwork (His workmanship),*
> *recreated in Christ Jesus, [born anew] that we may do those*
> *good works which God predestined (planned beforehand) for us*
> *[taking paths which He prepared ahead of time], that we should*
> *walk in them [living the good life which He prearranged and*
> *made ready for us to live].*" **Ephesians 2:10 (AMP)**

Building Your Financial Home Together

> *"Can two people walk together without agreeing on
> the direction?"* **Amos 3:3 (NLT)**

So many married couples have a hard time coming into agreement with the concept of oneness. Each one of them has their own agenda and future plan, which often times does not include their mate. So much more can be accomplished when a man and his wife walk in agreement. Jesus said in Matthew 18:19 **(NIV)**

> *"Again, I tell you that if two of you on earth agree about
> anything you ask for. It will be done for you by my Father
> in heaven."*

Although the scripture does not specify who the "two" should be, why would you not stand in agreement with your spouse on the things that would affect your family? Sure your friend Kim or Ron can stand in agreement with you. However, don't neglect the power of agreement that God had in mind with regards to your marriage.

God wants the commitment that the two of you made on your wedding day (to withstand the trials of life) to remain rooted within you to fulfill His will. In order to execute the plans that He intended for your union you must be in His will.

Team Building

This section addresses the scriptural principles of unity within your marriage according to the Word of God. Unity in the institution of marriage is a vital element to Christian marriages. God greatly desires that a man and his wife experience harmony and oneness with each other that he gave attention to it in his Word.

> *"Be eager and strive earnestly to guard and keep the harmony and
> oneness of [and produced by] the Spirit in the binding power of
> peace."* **Ephesians 4:3 (AMP)**

What do you think are some barriers that keep couples from working together on their finances? _____

_____

_____

_____

_____

_____

The Master's Plan For Your Master Suite

"And the Lord God said, 'It is not good for the man to be alone. I will make a helper suitable for him.' . . . So the Lord God caused the man to fall into a deep sleep; and while he was sleeping, He took one of the man's ribs and closed up the place with flesh. Then the Lord God made a woman from the rib (side) he had taken out of the man, and he brought her to the man." **Genesis 2:18, 21 22 (NIV)**

The Lord put the two of you together knowing that you are suitable helpers for each other. You are the perfect team to carry out His plans. God knows your financial needs, and He definitely knows that money is needed to fulfill your duties for the Kingdom. I once heard a well-known coach say, "It's easy to find good players; it's difficult getting them to play together." I believe that God feels the same way. It is easy to find a good man and a good woman to join in holy matrimony but it is difficult to get them to work as a team. God put the two of you together for a purpose. I believe that He created you both with a divine plan in mind.

"Furthermore, because we are united with Christ, we have received an inheritance from God, for he chose us in advance, and he makes everything work out according to his plan." **Ephesians 1:11 (NLT)**

There are four truths that will help you understand His plans:

➤ He put you together for a purpose.
"My prayer is that light will flood your hearts and that you will understand the hope that was given to you when God chose you. Then you will discover the glorious blessings that will be yours together with all of God's people." **Ephesians 1:18 (CEV)**

➤ You both are vital.
"A spiritual gift is given to each of us so we can help each other." **1Corinthians 12:7 (NLT)**

➤ God wants you to live in peace with one another.
"God blesses those who work for peace, for they will be called the children of God." **Matthew 5:9 (NLT)**

➤ God saved and chose you to be part of His plan.
"It is He who saved us and chose us for His holy work, not because we deserve it, but because that was His plan." **2 Timothy 1:9 (LB)**

Satan, you are NOT a part of this building process!

Jesus said:

> *"Yes, I am the gate. Those who come in through me will*
> *be saved. They will come and go freely and will find good*
> *pastures. The thief's purpose is to steal and destroy. My*
> *purpose is to give them a rich and satisfying life."* **John 10:9-10 (Amp)**

During this building process we do not need a wrecking ball on site, so who made Satan (a.k.a. the thief) part of the work-crew? Many couples will contract work out to Satan, as a result, homes are destroyed or left unfinished. According to a recent poll, *"financial stress is still reported, statistically, as being the leading cause of divorce"*. Couples need to know that God equipped us with all tools necessary to rise above our situations and circumstances, and we definitely don't have to look to Satan for help.

> *"Use every piece of God's armor to resist the enemy*
> *in the time of evil, so that after the battle you will still*
> *be standing firm"* **Ephesians 6:13 (NLT)**

The Word of God warns us:

> *"Stay alert! Watch out for your great enemy, the devil.*
> *He prowls around like a roaring lion, looking for someone*
> *to devour. Stand firm against him, and be strong in your*
> *faith. Remember that your Christian brothers and sisters*
> *all over the world are going through the same kind of*
> *suffering you are. In his kindness God called you to share*
> *in His eternal glory by means of Christ Jesus. So after you*
> *have suffered a little while, He will restore, support, and*
> *strengthen you, and He will place you on a firm foundation.*
> *All power to Him forever! Amen."* **1 Peter 5:8-11 (NLT)**

God knows that we all will have times of trials and a little suffering, but He made us four promises in 1 Peter 5:8-11. List them below:

1 _____
2 _____
3 _____
4 _____

PINK SLIP

Date_____

Mr. Satan,

We, _____ & _____ are no longer in need of your services. Please take all of your equipment and NEVER return to this work site again.

Sincerely Yours,

The _____

Please declare this:

Satan, we recognize who you are and what you are trying to do. We stand in agreement and declare that you are incapable of defeating us in our marriage, our family and our finances. We declare that ALL of your efforts are ineffective in stopping us from filling God's will for our family. We claim victory as we work together. In Jesus name!

***********************BUILDING BLOCKS**********************

<u>Deuteronomy 32:30</u> (NLT)

"How could one person chase a thousand of them, and two people put ten thousand to flight..."

<u>1 Corinthians 1:10</u> (NCV)

"I beg you, brothers and sisters, by the name of our Lord Jesus Christ that all of you agree with each other and not be split into groups. I beg that you be completely joined together by having the same kind of thinking and the same purpose."

<u>John 13:35</u> (NLT)

"Your love for one another will prove to the world that you are my disciples."

<u>Psalm 37:4</u> (ESV)

"Delight yourself in the LORD and he will give you the desires of your heart."

<u>Psalm 35:27</u> (KJV)

"Let them shout for joy, and be glad, that favour my righteous cause: yea, let them say continually, Let the LORD be magnified, which hath pleasure in the prosperity of his servant."

<u>Ephesians 2:10</u> (NLT)

"For we are God's masterpiece. He has created us anew in Christ Jesus, so we can do the good things He planned for us long ago.

********************SAY IT & CREATE IT********************

Confession: (confession regarding teamwork in your marriage)

"God, we thank you that we are graced to work together as a couple in the area of financial stewardship. We better understand the importance of being one mind with you and the importance of working together. We embrace a mindset of oneness, realizing that according to Amos 3:3 that we cannot move forward in our future together without a commitment to walk together. Father teach us to trust one another, knowing that your Word says that there is no fear in perfect love (1 John 4:18). We declare that our love has been made perfect through You.

Satan we are now able to recognize your works. We render you powerless in our finances and will no longer allow you to keep us in the dark regarding the great plans that the Lord has in store for our marriage.

We declare victory in working together! In Jesus Name"

NOTES

_____
_____
_____
_____
_____
_____
_____
_____
_____
_____
_____
_____
_____
_____
_____
_____

WHO HELPED IN MOLDING YOUR MONEY MANAGEMENT TENDENCIES?

Check all that apply:

HIS		HERS
_____	My Dad	_____
_____	My Mom	_____
_____	A Relative(s)	_____
_____	A Friend(s)	_____
_____	School	_____
_____	Trial and Error (self)	_____
_____	Church	_____
_____	Other _____	_____
_____	Life Experiences	_____

1. What were some good money management habits that were learned from those above?

His: _____

_____

Hers: _____

_____

2. What were some bad habits that were learned?

His: _____

_____

Hers: _____

_____

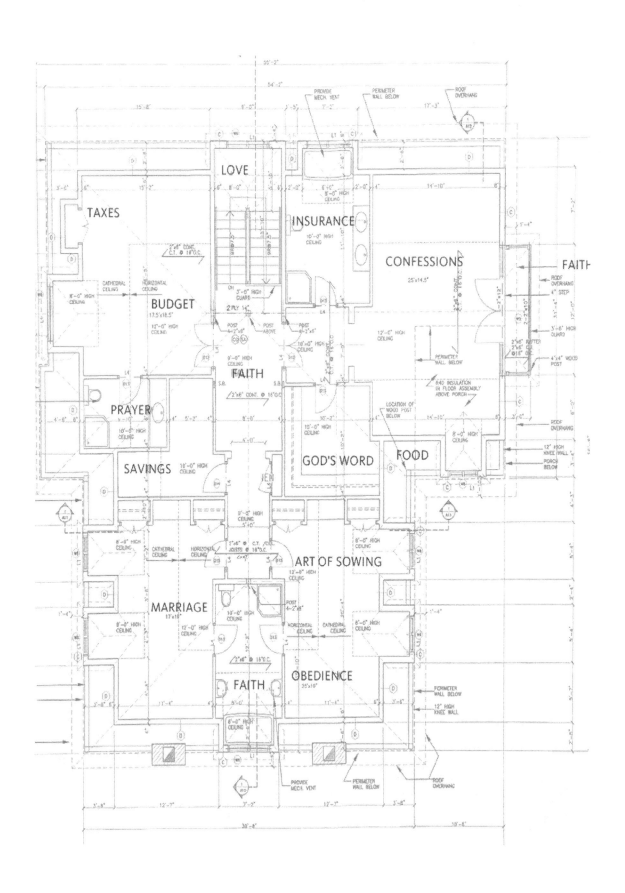

PHASE 2

DESIGNING THE BLUEPRINTS

Phase 2

Designing the Blueprints

Building Principle:

Be willing, obedient and follow God's plan.

Memory Verse:

"For I know the plans I have for you, declares the Lord, plans to prosper and not harm you, plans to give you hope and a future" **Jeremiah 29:11(NIV)**

Overview

The purpose of this phase is to teach you important principles of designing your financial home. Take the image of your financial home and make it a reality in your life. You can start by visualizing it in your mind's eye and seeing God's part in it, knowing that He has great things in store for you and your family.

Building Objectives:

➤ Understanding the importance of God's Word in your building process.
➤ How to use God's Word to mold the images of your plans.
➤ Understanding how your needs, wants and desires affect your plans.
➤ Declaring God's word over your plans.

Understanding God's Plan

The Word of God should be the first "how-to-book" that Christians should run to for almost every aspect of life. Why are people so eager to seek advice from this world's system before seeking the wisdom that comes from the Bible? Would you consider calling the makers of Toyota to inquire about malfunctions that you're having with your new Ford? Is it possible for Toyota to advise you on your problems? Of course, they can try. However, the makers of Ford would definitely handle your needs more effectively. Likewise, God Almighty, the Creator of life is most qualified to advise us on how to live, cultivate successful relationships, and properly manage our finances.

There are thousands of references to money in the Bible, and most of Jesus' parables dealt with the use of money. Finances have been a major battle within the lives of God's people for far too long. Satan has succeeded in past battles but it's time for the Body of Christ to choose the Word of God as their weapon of choice in this war, and defeat the enemy once and for all.

So, often you will hear a believer say, "I believe in God", but do you believe Him? In other words, do you have faith in Him and His promises?

We are even reminded on U.S. currency "In God We Trust". The Word of God encourages us to:

> *"Trust in the Lord with all thine heart and lean not unto thine own understanding. In all thy ways acknowledge Him and He shall direct thy path".* **Proverbs 3:5-6 (KJV)**

Let us have faith and trust in God to gain the wisdom and knowledge needed to defeat the enemy and escape his countless attacks. God's principles of financial stewardship are what He intended for us to equip ourselves with to conquer financial warfare and ultimately understand His plan. How can we experience the Blessings of God if we don't understand His plan?

This phase is designed to help you identify some of God's principles of financial stewardship and to help you develop successful plans for prospering according to the Word of God. He wants us to use the wisdom that comes from Him to develop the blueprints for the construction of our financial homes. What image of your financial home has God given you?

*********** Let's begin building! ************

Your Home Starts With An Image

We have God's creative powers working in us to help us see ourselves the same way that God sees us. An imagination full of successful endeavors and witty ideas are gifts from God. We have to recognize the importance of lining our thinking up with His promises. Our minds then become canvases for the images that God wants us to have of ourselves — images of rising to new heights and total life prosperity. Often believers fail to recognize the Lord's awesome powers that are working in us, and how He is trying to move in our lives. Isaiah 43:19 (NLT) says:

> *"For I am about to do something new. See, I have already*
> *begun! Do you not see it? I will make a pathway through*
> *the wilderness. I will create rivers in the dry wasteland."*

God wants us to get a clear image of His life changing abilities. He wants us to know that He has already done His part; the rest is up to us. Start now believing what God has to say about you and trust Him to rebuild images that you have of yourself, your marriage and your finances. Get rid of the images of fear, doubt and unbelief that are standing between you and God's best for your life. Step out on faith and start pursuing your heart's desires.

> *"Summing it all up, friends, I'd say you'll do best by filling your minds*
> *and meditating on things true, noble, reputable, authentic, compelling,*
> *gracious – the best , not the worst; the beautiful, not the ugly; things*
> *to praise, not things to curse. Put into practice what you learned from*
> *me, what you heard and saw and realized. Do that, and God, who*
> *makes everything work together, will work you into His most excellent*
> *harmonies."* **Philippians 4:8-9 (MSG)**

Making Those Images a Reality

What images has God been placing in you? Let's sketch in all the details by identifying your financial needs, want and desires. God will not only give you the vision but He will also provide you with the blueprint, details and strategies needed to execute the construction of those plans. All three are instrumental to the building process. They serve as driving forces that allow your images of your home to take form. It is unusual for an architect to verbally submit his or her blueprints to a builder. His plans must be drawn out to avoid leaving out details. Can you imagine living in your physical home without a kitchen, simply because the architect forgot to tell the builder to include one? Or because the builder forgot that the architect said to put a kitchen in. The blueprints are key resources needed to convey the architect's DESIGN, and to ensure that the builder and the rest of the crew bring his image to reality. The key, however, is to be Kingdom minded and to commit your plans to the Lord.

Below are seven steps for successful goal setting:

1. <u>GOALS:</u> Begin to see yourself as God sees you.
> *"It's in Christ that we find out who we are and what we are living for.*
> *Long before we first heard of Christ and got our hopes up, He had*
> *His eye on us, had designs on us for glorious living, part of the over*
> *all purpose He is working out in everything and everyone"* **Ephesians 1:11 (MSG)**

2. <u>PUT YOUR PLANS INTO ACTION:</u> Do your part.
> *"For as the body without the spirit is dead, so faith without works is dead also."*
> **James 2:26 (NKJV)**

> ➤ Imagine the possibilities
> ➤ Write them down
> ➤ Determine your action plans (implement strategies)

3. <u>STATE YOUR PURPOSE.</u> What benefit does this goal have on your finances?
> *"The purposes of a man's heart are deep waters, but a man of understanding*
> *draws them out."* **Proverbs 20:5 (NIV)**

4. <u>AVOID PROCRASTINATING.</u> Now is always a good time!
> *"Teach us to use wisely all the time we have."* **Psalm 90:12 (CEV)**

5. <u>TIMING.</u> Establish a timeline. However, be patient.
> *"At the time I have decided, my words will come true. You can trust*
> *what I say about the future. It may take a long time, but keep on*
> *waiting-- it will happen!"* **Habakkuk 2:3 (CEV)**

> ➤ Short term (ST) – less than 1 year to achieve.
> ➤ Intermediate term (IT) – that which can be accomplished within a five-year period.
> ➤ Long term (LT) – goals that will take more than five years to achieve.

6. <u>CONFESS SCRIPTURES:</u> Find encouragement in God's Word.
   Here is the missing link that many Christians leave out: God's promises, which serve as the nuts and bolts in this building process. Take time to study his Word and speak it over your plans. God's Word is so full of encouragement. You must start looking at your life through God's promises and with eyes of faith. It's up to you to take the time and search the scriptures and find out what He says.

7. <u>HAVE FAITH:</u> Trust God with your plans.
> *"Commit to the Lord whatever you do, and your plans will*
> *succeed."* **Proverbs 16:3 (NIV)**

Our Family Vision Plan

God's Word encourages us to write the vision. Please take time to sit down as a family and write out the vision that God has given you for your family. *Custom Built* was titled as such to remind couples that God has a specially tailored plan for your family. While you and the "Jones" may have similar plans, your plans should not and will not be their plans and vice versa. This exercise is a key component to accomplishing the custom design that God intended especially for your family.

_____
_____
_____
_____
_____
_____
_____
_____
_____
_____
_____
_____
_____
_____
_____
_____
_____
_____
_____
_____
_____
_____
_____
_____
_____
_____
_____
_____
_____
_____
_____

PROSPERITY PLANS

GOALS	SETTING PRIORITIES	TIMING	REVIEWING/ ACCOMPLISHED (CHECK R OR A)	SCRIPTURE(S)
Bugeting_____ _____ _____ _____ Action Plan(s)_____ _____ _____ _____	❑ Important ❑ Very Important ❑ Extremely Important	❑ ST ❑ IT ❑ LT	❑ (R) Date____ ❑ (A) Date____ ❑ _____ ❑ _____	_____ _____ _____ _____ _____ _____
Savings_____ _____ _____ _____ Action Plan(s)_____ _____ _____ _____	❑ Important ❑ Very Important ❑ Extremely Important	❑ ST ❑ IT ❑ LT	❑ (R) Date____ ❑ (A) Date____ ❑ _____ ❑ _____	_____ _____ _____ _____ _____ _____
Debt Cancellation_____ _____ _____ _____ Action Plan(s)_____ _____ _____ _____	❑ Important ❑ Very Important ❑ Extremely Important	❑ ST ❑ IT ❑ LT	❑ (R) Date____ ❑ (A) Date____ ❑ _____ ❑ _____	_____ _____ _____ _____ _____ _____
Ministry_____ _____ _____ _____ Action Plan(s)_____ _____ _____ _____	❑ Important ❑ Very Important ❑ Extremely Important	❑ ST ❑ IT ❑ LT	❑ (R) Date____ ❑ (A) Date____ ❑ _____ ❑ _____	_____ _____ _____ _____ _____ _____

ST - Short Term
IT - Intermediate Term
LT - Long Term

PROSPERITY PLANS

GOALS	SETTING PRIORITIES	TIMING	REVIEWED/ ACCOMPLISHED (CHECK R OR A)	SCRIPTURES(S)
Retirement_____ _____ _____ _____ Action Plan(s)_____ _____ _____ _____	❑ Important ❑ Very Important ❑ Extremely Important	❑ ST ❑ IT ❑ LT	❑ (R) Date_____ ❑ (A) Date_____ ❑ _____ ❑ _____	
Giving_____ _____ _____ _____ Action Plan(s)_____ _____ _____ _____	❑ Important ❑ Very Important ❑ Extremely Important	❑ ST ❑ IT ❑ LT	❑ (R) Date_____ ❑ (A) Date_____ ❑ _____ ❑ _____	
Educational_____ _____ _____ _____ Action Plan(s)_____ _____ _____ _____	❑ Important ❑ Very Important ❑ Extremely Important	❑ ST ❑ IT ❑ LT	❑ (R) Date_____ ❑ (A) Date_____ ❑ _____ ❑ _____	
Investments_____ _____ _____ _____ Action Plan(s)_____ _____ _____ _____	❑ Important ❑ Very Important ❑ Extremely Important	❑ ST ❑ IT ❑ LT	❑ (R) Date_____ ❑ (A) Date_____ ❑ _____ ❑ _____	

ST - Short Term
IT - Intermediate Term
LT - Long Term

Share valuable principles that you have learned from this phase that will help in your building process.

_____

_____

_____

_____

_____

***************************Building Blocks*****************************

Ephesians 3:20 (NCV)
"With God's power working in us, God can do much, much more than anything we can ask or imagine."

Psalm 20:4 (NIV)
"May He give you the desire of your heart and make all your plans succeed."

Proverbs 23:7 (NASB)
"For as he thinks within himself, so he is…"

Psalm 37:5 (KJV)
"Commit thy way unto the LORD; trust also in him; and he shall bring it to pass."

Mark 9:23 (NKJV)
"… all things are possible for him who believes."

Ephesians 4:22-23 (AMP)
"Strip yourselves of your former nature…and be constantly renewed in the spirit of your mind [having a fresh mental and spiritual attitude].

Hebrews 10:35 (NLT)

"So do not throw away this confident trust in the Lord. Remember the great reward it brings you!"

Proverbs 21:5 (NIV)

"The plans of the diligent lead to profit as surely as haste leads to poverty."

*************************SAY IT & CREATE IT**********************

Confession:

"We embrace the mindset of endless possibilities. We refuse to let the world dictate who we are and all that we can be. We see ourselves as God sees us. We have faith in His promises, and we are determined to set our thinking according to His Word. We thank you Father that we are predestined to live the good life, and for your plans of prosperity for our family (Psa 115:14). We present to you our goals and dreams knowing that it was you that placed those great images in us. As your righteous people we do not walk in fear, but in faith and great expectation that you will grant us our desires (Prov 10:24), In Jesus name!

NOTES

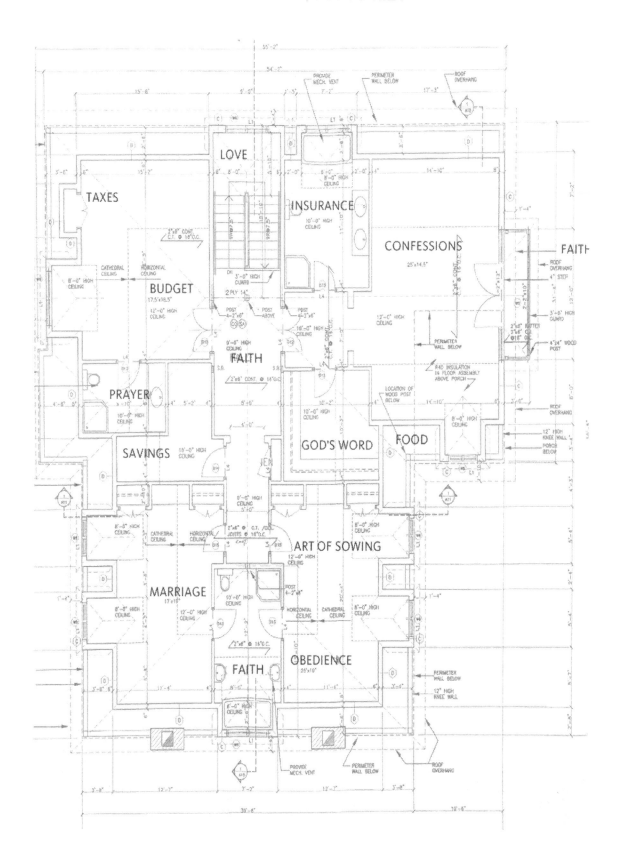

PHASE 3

LAYING A SOLID FOUNDATION

Phase 3

Laying a Solid Foundation

Building Principle:

Financial planning God's way must be built and maintained on a strong foundation.

Memory Verse:

"And the rains descended, and the floods came, and the winds blew, and beat upon that house; and it fell not: for it was founded upon a rock" **Matthew 7:25 (KJV)**

Overview

This phase covers the importance of building your financial home on the foundation of sound financial principles and promises that are only found in the Word of God. As stewards, His Word provides us with guidelines for managing the money He has entrusted us with. These guidelines are also essential for unity within marriages. Whether you are engaged, newlyweds or married for a significant number of years, God's Word provides a foundation that's able to withstand any financial storm.

Building Objectives:

> Building your foundation.
> Seeking wisdom from God's Word.
> Applying biblical principles to your financial plan.
> Building a financial plan based on God's promises.

Building Your Foundation

"Why do you call me, 'Lord, Lord,' and do not do what I say? I will show you what he is like who comes to me and hears my words and puts them into practice. He is like a man building a house, who dug down deep and laid the foundation on rock. When a flood came, the torrent struck that house but could not shake it, because it was well built." **Luke 6:46-48 (NIV)**

The parables of The Wise and Foolish Builders are located in both the book of Matthew and Luke. These parables give you a vivid description of the advantages of being a wise disciple of Jesus Christ. It helps you to rely on and practice wisdom that only comes from the Word of God.

At the base of any strong structure rests a strategically planned and well-constructed foundation. It is amazing that this concept seems logical, however many people often disregard the obvious and build their lives on foolish teachings. This parable can be seen as a reflection in all aspects of life, proving the importance of exercising God's wisdom in our families, our businesses, our relationships and our finances. As believers, we have to consider every aspect of our lives and choose God's Word as the foundation. We should not spend countless years building a financial tower (or any other aspect of life) on false appearances only hoping and wishing that it would stand during trying times. Instead, we should build based on the firm foundation of Christ and not look to the world as a basis for hope.

There are three important keys to consider when establishing your foundation.

> ➤ Apply His Principles.
> ➤ Take hold of His covenant promises.
> ➤ Have faith in His Word.

Joshua 1:8 says,

"This book of the Law shall not depart from your mouth, but you shall meditate in it day and night, that you may observe to do according to all that is written in it. For then you will make your way prosperous, and then you will have good success. **(NKJV)**

The Principle in Joshua 1:8 is _____
And as a result two promises are made:
That you will _____ and
then you will _____.

Now it's up to you to have faith in God's unfailing Word.

In the 3 John 2 **(KJV)** we are reminded,

> *"Beloved, I wish above all things that thou mayest prosper*
> *and be in health, even as thy soul* prospereth."

   This scripture wishes that we should prosper and be in health. It appears that there is a direct connection to financial prosperity, health and the prosperity of our soul. Plainly stated, you must be grounded in His Word in order to live in true prosperity. When you accept that it is God's will for you to prosper and you are obedient to His Word by applying his principles, then you are ready to receive his best.

Jesus said to his disciples:

> *"...To you has been entrusted the mystery of the kingdom*
> *of God [that is, the secret counsels of God which are hidden*
> *from the ungodly]; but for those outside [of our circle] every*
> *thing becomes a parable,"* **Mark 4:11 (AMP)**

   As believers, we should capture the attention of the non-believers as they marvel over how we prosper in every area of our lives. Unfortunately, the world's way of doing things has been adapted by many believers. They have fallen into the same "rat-race" that stresses the unbelievers.

> *"If our Message is obscure to anyone, it's not because*
> *we're holding back in any way. No, it's because these*
> *other people are looking or going the wrong way and*
> *refuse to give it serious attention. All they have eyes for*
> *is the fashionable god of darkness. They think he can give*
> *them what they want, and that they won't have to bother*
> *believing a Truth they can't see. They're stone-blind to the*
> *dayspring brightness of the Message that shines with*
> *Christ, who gives us the best picture of God we'll ever get.*
> **2 Corinthians 4: 3-4 (MSG)**

   As children of the Most High God, we should not be blinded and be misled by the world's system. We should walk in the Light of God and follow His plan for our lives.

> *"Understanding Your word brings light to the minds of*
> *ordinary people."* **Psalm 119:130 (CEV)**

Matching

Building Verses

_____ *"The wicked borrows and does never repay…"*
Psalm 37:21 (NLT)

_____ *"Trust in the Lord with all thine heart: and lean not unto thine own understanding."* **Proverbs 3:5(KJV)**

_____ *"If you have not been faithful in the use of that which is another's, who will give you that which is your own?"* **Luke 16:12 (KJV)**

_____ *"The rich rules over the poor, and the borrower is servant to the lender."* **Proverbs 22:7 (KJV)**

_____ *"Dishonest money dwindles away, but he who gathers money little by little makes it grow.* **Proverbs 13:11 (NIV)**

_____ *"Two are better than one because they have a good [more satisfying] return for their labor."* **Eccelesiastes 4:9 (AMP)**

_____ *"It is not wise to promise to pay what your neighbor owes."* **Proverbs 17:18 (NCV)**

_____ *"But this I say, He which soweth sparingly shall reap also sparingly; and he which soweth bountifully shall reap also bountifully."* **2 Corinthians 9:6 (KJV)**

Principles

A. Avoid cosigning

B. There are benefits to making decisions together

C. It is evil to borrow and never repay

D. Have great faith and trust in the guidance of the Lord

E. Avoid debt because the borrower is subject to the authority of the lender

F. Whatever you sow is what you're going to reap

G. If you don't properly care for someone else's property, you will never own your own

H. Earn an honest living

God's Word is full of His covenant promises. Read the scripture passages below and write down what is promised us in each one.

What's the Promise?

Luke 6:31-38

_____
_____
_____

Psalm 37:4

_____
_____
_____

Isaiah 1:19

_____
_____
_____

2 Corinthians 9:6

_____
_____
_____

What specific promise(s) from God's Word do you believe Him for?

Scripture: _____

The promise:

_____
_____
_____
_____

Scripture: _____

The promise:

_____
_____
_____
_____

**************************BUILDING BLOCKS*************************

James 2:22 (NIV)
"*You see that his faith and his actions were working together, and his faith was made complete by what he did.*"

Romans 4:16 (NIV)
"*Therefore, the promise comes by faith, so that it may be by grace and may be guaranteed to all Abraham's offspring—not only to those who are of the law but also to those who are of the faith of Abraham. He is the father of us all.*"

1 Corinthians 2:5 (ESV)
"*so that your faith might not rest on men's wisdom, but on God's power.*

Acts 27:25 (NIV)
"*So keep up your courage, men, for I have faith in God that it will happen just as he told me.*"

***********************SAY IT AND CREATE IT***********************

Confession: (write your personal faith confession over your financial home)

God we are thankful that You have provided us with your Word as a means of guidance…

_____
_____
_____
_____
_____
_____
_____
_____

NOTES

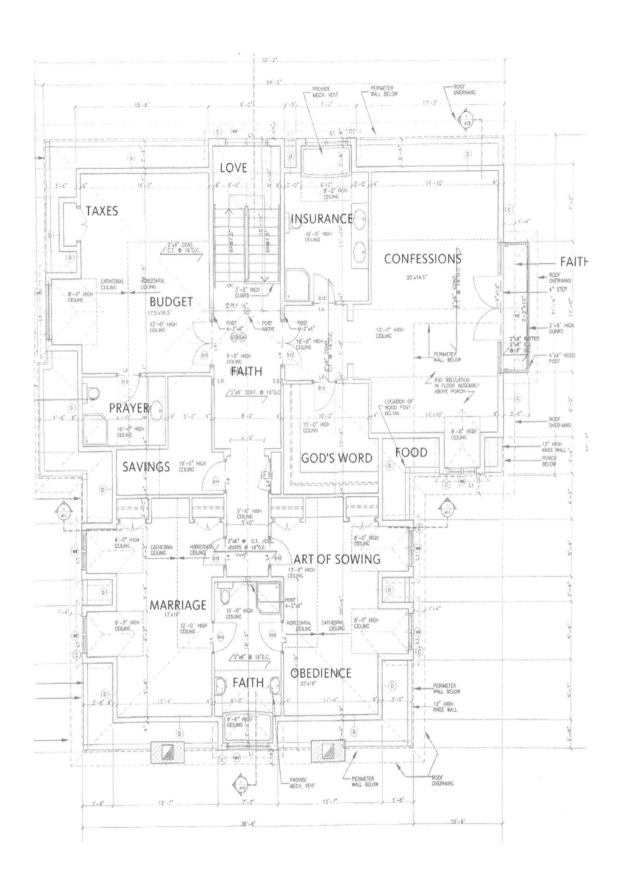

PHASE 4

BUILDING YOUR FRAMEWORK

Phase 4

Building Your Framework

Building Principle:

Know where you are financially.

Memory Verse:

"Know the state of your flocks, and put your heart into caring for your herds" **Proverbs 27:23 (NLT)**

Overview

Phase four will help you to locate where you are financially in your building process. The tools offered in this phase will help you to clearly bring your current financial standing into focus and provide you with the measurements needed to begin building. Whether it is a new construction or a renovation, this phase will help you get a clearer picture of your design, identify what you want to accomplish and help you focus on where to concentrate your efforts. It is important not to avoid these topics because the framework is a vital component that is needed to support your "home".

Building Objectives:

> ➢ Inspecting Your Credit History
> ➢ Calculating Your Net Worth
> ➢ Creating a Spending Plan
> ➢ Understanding the Tithe
> ➢ Making Adjustments

Credit Inspections

The heart of a believer is examined when it comes to credit and God is concerned with your level of integrity.

According to His Word:

> *"The wicked borrow and does not pay back, but the righteous is gracious and gives."*
> **Psalm 37:21 (NAS)**

In this scripture the wicked is described as one who…? _____

Another scripture says:

> *"The rich rule over the poor, and the borrower is a servant to the lender"* **Proverbs 22:7 (KJV)**

I am reminded of a tale told in one of my favorite books, *The Richest Man In Babylon*. The tale is about a man's experience with debt. In the book, he shares how his desire for material things ruined his relationships with his family, friends and creditors, ultimately causing him to be sold into slavery. He found himself like much of society, "spinning uncontrollably in a whirlwind of trouble and humiliation" as he realized that his income could no longer support his lifestyle and his debt.

Borrowing is not a sin but God's Word warns us of the consequences of accumulating great debt. In fact, God intended for us His children, to be the lenders and not borrowers. In order for this to come to pass faith in His Word is required.

> *"The Lord shall open to you His good treasury, the heavens, to give the rain of your land **in its season** and to bless all the work of your hands; and you shall lend to many nations, but you shall not borrow."* **Deuteronomy 28:12**

The way you handle your financial obligations says a lot about you. Make a decision to protect the integrity of your name and your credit. In Proverbs 22:1 **(NIV)**, we are reminded that

> *"A good name is to be more desired than great wealth, to be esteemed is better than silver and gold"*

As believers, we should not be overly concerned with acquiring great material wealth when we do not have the financial ability to do so. We should not rely on credit to acquire material possessions. We should rely on God instead and have faith in His covenant promises and His timing for releasing His blessings over us.

10 Techniques to help you manage your credit wisely

1. Pay your bills on time. **(Romans 13:8)**
    *this will help raise your credit score, avoid high interest rates and late fees.

2. Thoroughly read over your bills each month. **(Proverbs 3:13)**
    *look for possible billing errors or billing mistakes. Most credit card companies will only give you 60 days to dispute errors.
3. Have a debt reduction plan. **(Romans 13:8)**
    *strive to pay off all debt every month. If it is not possible try to pay off debt as soon as possible.
4. Optimally, keep your total account balance at or about 75% of your total available credit.
5. If you have had problems managing your accounts, contact your creditors or a reliable credit-counseling agency to help re-establish your credit history. **(Proverbs 11:14)**
6. Negotiate with your creditors to lower your interest rates.
7. Read the fine print and beware of unnecessary extras: **(Proverbs 4:7)**
    -annual fees
    -credit insurance
    -over the limit fees
    -fixed or variable interest rate
    -term charges
8. Avoid co-signing for anyone **(Proverbs 6:1-3)**
9. Annually review what appears on your credit report and learn what your current FICO (credit) score is. **(Proverbs 27:23)**
10. Protect your identity from being stolen.

It is vital to review your credit report by contacting the national credit reporting agencies:

- Equifax   800-685-1111 or www.equifax.com
- Experian   888-397-3742 or www.experian.com
- Trans Union   800-888-4213 or www.transunion.com

OR

Visit www.annualcreditreport.com for all three

Building good credit and maintaining it requires work on your part.

"For as the human body apart from the spirit is lifeless, so faith apart from [its] works of obedience is also dead." **James 2:26 (AMP)**

List of Debts

Account Name, Acct Number, Contact Information	Current Balance	Interest Rate	Number of Remaining Payments	Monthly Payments	Date Due	Status

Wealth Assessment

You were encouraged in your memory verse to *"Know well the condition of your flocks, and put your heart into caring for your herd."* **Proverbs 27:23 (NLT)** During biblical days wealth was identified by livestock and land....

How does this scripture relate to wealth as we currently know it today?

_____
_____
_____

ASSETS (what you own)		LIABILITIES (what you owe)	
Cash:		**Personal Loans:**	
Cash	_____	Family/Friends	_____
Checking Acct.	_____	Educational	_____
Savings Acct.	_____	Financial Institutions	_____
Money Market	_____		_____
Cash Value of Life Insurance	_____	Life Insurance	_____
Other:	_____		
Personal Property:			
Personal Residence	_____	Mortgage Loan(s)	_____
Vacation Home	_____	Vacation Mortgage	_____
Automobile(s)	_____	Automobile Loan (s)	_____
Collectibles	_____	Other:	_____
Jewelry/Furs	_____	Other:	_____
Recreational Vehicle(s)	_____		
Investments:		**Current Debts:**	
Certificate(s) of Deposit	_____	Medical	_____
Mutual Funds	_____	Credit Card(s)	_____
401(k), 403(b)...	_____	Department Store	_____
Pension Plans	_____	IRS	_____
Stocks	_____	Other:	_____
Bonds	_____	Other:	_____
Annuities	_____		
Business:			
Fair Market Value	_____	Business Liability	_____
Real Estate Value	_____		
Other:			
_____	_____	_____	_____

47

In the financial service world this assessment is referred to as your "net worth". Please understand that your wealth does not determine your worth to God. 1 Peter 1:18-19 (CEV) is one of many scriptures that reaffirm your true value.

"You were rescued from the useless way of life that you learned from your ancestors. But you know that you were not rescued by such things as silver or gold that don't last forever. You were rescued by the precious blood of Christ, that spotless and innocent lamb."

The Message translation of verse 18 reads:

"Your life is a journey you must travel with a deep consciousness of God. It cost God plenty to get you out of that dead-end, empty-headed life you grew up in. He paid with Christ's sacred blood, you know."

Regardless of your current financial state, your "true" net worth is summed up in how valuable you are to God. This survey is simply a tool that can be used to give you a snap shot of where you are and serve as a guide for expansion. You then develop plans for increasing your assets and decreasing your liabilities.

As the righteousness of God it is time for us to take dominion over our finances, and take our rightful authority over the things of this world and stop letting "things" control us.

Set some time aside as a family and pray over your finances. Ask God to show you how to be better stewards, then learn how to successfully control your money and avoid letting your money control you.

<u>When money controls:</u>

> ➤ Your needs, wants and desires become unclear
> ➤ You don't make wise purchasing decisions
> ➤ You constantly worry about paying bills
> ➤ Your desire to give to others is halted by your financial circumstances
> ➤ You take unnecessary financial risks
> ➤ You borrow without realistically knowing how to pay it back
> ➤ You compromise your values to get it (lie, cheat, steal…)
> ➤ Your mood is based on your finances
> ➤ You spend money to make you feel better
> ➤ You make excuses for not sowing into God's Kingdom, or you give in fear
> ➤ And the list goes on…

As a family, identify ways that money controls you. A part of your building process is to take that control back. First, start by distinguishing between your needs, wants and desires and then discipline yourself to live within your means. Utilize basic tools and strategies to assist you with building a plan of prosperity such as: budget forms, savings calculators, expense tracking logs and accountability partners to name a few.

The "B" Word

It's time to find out what the Word of God has to say about that dreaded "B" word, BUDGET. Yes, true financial stewardship does involve budgeting. Luke 14:28-29 **(NCV)** says:

"If you want to build a tower, you first sit down and decide how much it will cost, to see if you have enough money to finish the job. If you don't, you might lay the foundation, but you would not be able to finish the job."

A "tower" may not be in your plans but you should work on building a sturdy financial home. Most people have little to no idea how much they spend each month which may be the cause of them constantly overspending and leaving them in a financial bind. A budget is a necessary tool for managing your finances.

"The blessings of the Lord, maketh rich, and He added no sorrow with it" **Proverbs 10:22 (ESV)**

God wants us to enjoy material blessings, not to fall prey to financial traps and be burdened by them month after month. Financial stress is prevalent in the lives of many Christians and is also one of the major causes of marital problems. This is definitely outside of the will of God. Jesus came to give us the more abundant life. It is an important principle for believers to learn that lack is not in God's plan for our lives. *"Those who seek the Lord will not lack any good thing"* **(Psalm 34:10)**. Following a budget provides a basis for accountability. You become empowered to take charge of your finances under the guidance of the Lord. Budgeting ushers us into the freedom we need to respond to the promptings of God (as oppose to being in bondage). As a result, we are able to receive the full manifestation of His promises there by fulfilling His will for our finances.

Let's inspect some possible code violations that might hinder your building process: **check all that may apply**

- ❑ little to no knowledge of God's Word
- ❑ living beyond your means
- ❑ lack of discipline
- ❑ impatience
- ❑ poor financial habits
- ❑ fear of lack
- ❑ little to no planning
- ❑ lack of sound counsel
- ❑ greed
- ❑ lack of contentment
- ❑ other:_____

Home Inspection

Paul and Kat Carter have been married for 8 years. They have two sons, PJ (7 y/o) and Caleb (5 y/o). Paul earns a living as a nurse and Kat works part-time at the local bank as a teller. Together the couple earns an income of $87,500 annually. They argue constantly about their finances and simply can't understand why they are having a hard time getting ahead in life. Four years ago, Paul's mother encouraged him to separate his income from Kat's. They now have two separate bank accounts and they both have bills that they are responsible for paying. The value of their home is $195,000 and they still owe $153,500. The Carters have two cars but only have one car payment. Paul's car is paid for. Although they live in a great school district, Paul insists that the boys go to a private school. They both see education as a priority, so the couple is currently funding an educational plan for the boys' future. Paul is contributing into his 401(k) at work but the couple feels that they cannot afford to make contributions into Kat's. Family time is important to them. The Carters take very nice vacations every year using their tax refund. They have not yet started an emergency fund. They rely heavily on credit when unexpected things in life happen. They have two maxed out credit cards totaling $7,500. Kat has two more lines of credit (at her favorite department stores) that Paul is unaware of; totaling about $1600. The family attends "The Church That God Built". They know with all their being that "God knows their heart" regarding their inability to tithe. Paul and Kat think about many goals that they would like to accomplish in life, but have never set any true goals nor discuss them in detail. The Carters then come to you for help; please review their budget on page 51. Record your recommendations for the couple below and recalculate their budget based upon your suggestions onto the blank budget form on page 52, with the goal of balancing their budget. Once you have completed the Carter's budget, use the blank budget form on page 53 for your household.

Recommendations_____

_____
_____
_____
_____
_____
_____
_____
_____
_____
_____
_____
_____
_____
_____
_____
_____
_____
_____
_____
_____

*** The Carter's Family Budget ***
MONTHLY INCOME AND EXPENSES

GROSS INCOME:

Salary	$ 5,833.60
Salary	$ 1,458.03
Child Support	$
Other:	$
Other:	$
TOTAL	$ 7,291.63

OPPORTUNITY TO PROSPER:

Tithes	$
Offering	$ 80.00
TOTAL (A)	$ 80.00

HOME EXPENSES:

Mortgage/Rent	$ 1,375.00
Electricity/Gas	$ 177.00
Water/Trash	$ 54.00
Phone/Internet	$ 75.00
Cable/satellite	$ 85.00
Groceries	$ 335.00
Furnishings	$
Lawn care	$ 190.00
Improvements	$
Cell Phones	$ 225.00
Insurance	$ 55.00
Pet Care	$
Subscriptions	$ 42.00
Other:	$
TOTAL (B)	$ 2,613.00

PERSONAL CARE EXPENSES:

Clothing	$ 55.00
Toiletries	$ 30.00
Barber/salon	$ 140.00
Life Insurance	$ 135.00
TOTAL (C)	$ 360.00

CHILDCARE EXPENSES:

Tuition	$ 975.00
Babysitting	$ 100.00
Child support	$
Sports/Rec.	$
TOTAL (D)	$ 1,075.00

SAVINGS:

Savings Account	$
Emergency fund	$
College savings	$ 140.00
Investments	$
Retirement	$ 175.00
Other:	$
TOTAL (E)	$ 315.00

OBLIGATIONS:

Student loans	$ 235.00
Taxes (Federal & State)	$ 1,375.00
Credit card	$ 90.00
Credit card	$ 95.00
Other:	$ 87.00
TOTAL (F)	$

TRANSPORTATION EXPENSES:

Vehicle payment	$ 230.00
Fuel	$ 367.00
License/registration	$ 15.00
Public transit	$
Insurance	$ 105.00
Maintenance	$
Other: car wash	$ 18.00
TOTAL (G)	$ 735.00

HEALTHCARE EXPENSES:

Office visits	$
Prescriptions (Rx)	$ 22.00
Health insurance	$ 245.00
Gym membership/sports	$ 65.00
Other:	$
TOTAL (H)	$ 332.00

ENTERTAINMENT EXPENSES:

TOTAL (I)	$ 85.00

CALCULATIONS

Total Gross Income:	$ 7,291.63
- (minus) Total Expenses (A-I) -	$ 7,477.00
= (equals) Surplus/Deficit	$ -185.37
	(surplus/deficit)

*** The Carter's Family Budget ***
MONTHLY INCOME AND EXPENSES

GROSS INCOME:
Salary	$ 5,833.60
Salary	$ 1,458.03
Child Support	$_____
Other:_____	$_____
Other:_____	$_____
TOTAL	$ 7,291.63

OPPORTUNITY TO PROSPER:
Tithes	$_____
Offering	$_____
TOTAL (A)	$_____

HOME EXPENSES:
Mortgage/Rent	$_____
Electricity/Gas	$_____
Water/Trash	$_____
Phone/Internet	$_____
Cable/satellite	$_____
Groceries	$_____
Furnishings	$_____
Lawn care	$_____
Improvements	$_____
Cell Phones	$_____
Insurance	$_____
Pet Care	$_____
Subscriptions	$_____
Other:_____	$_____
TOTAL (B)	$_____

PERSONAL CARE EXPENSES:
Clothing	$_____
Toiletries	$_____
Barber/salon	$_____
Life Insurance	$_____
TOTAL (C)	$_____

CHILDCARE EXPENSES:
Tuition	$_____
Babysitting	$_____
Child support	$_____
Sports/Rec.	$_____
TOTAL (D)	$_____

SAVINGS:
Savings Account	$_____
Emergency fund	$_____
College savings	$_____
Investments	$_____
Retirement	$_____
Other:_____	$_____
TOTAL (E)	$_____

OBLIGATIONS:
Student loans	$_____
Taxes (Federal & State)	$_____
	$_____
Credit card	$_____
Credit card	$_____
Other:_____	$_____
TOTAL (F)	$_____

TRANSPORTATION EXPENSES:
Vehicle payment	$_____
Fuel	$_____
License/registration	$_____
Public transit	$_____
Insurance	$_____
Maintenance	$_____
Other:_____	$_____
TOTAL (G)	$_____

HEALTHCARE EXPENSES:
Office visits	$_____
Prescriptions (Rx)	$_____
Health insurance	$_____
Gym membership/sports	$_____
Other:_____	$_____
TOTAL (H)	$_____

ENTERTAINMENT EXPENSES:
TOTAL (I)	$_____

CALCULATIONS
Total Gross Income:	$_____
-(minus) Total Expenses (A-I)	-$_____
= (equals)	$_____
	(surplus/deficit)

*** Your Family Budget ***
MONTHLY INCOME AND EXPENSES

GROSS INCOME:
Salary	$_____
Salary	$_____
Child Support	$_____
Other:_____	$_____
Other:_____	$_____
TOTAL	$_____

OPPORTUNITY TO PROSPER:
Tithes	$_____
Offering	$_____
TOTAL (A)	$_____

HOME EXPENSES:
Mortgage/Rent	$_____
Electricity/Gas	$_____
Water/Trash	$_____
Phone/Internet	$_____
Cable/satellite	$_____
Groceries	$_____
Furnishings	$_____
Lawn care	$_____
Improvements	$_____
Cell Phones	$_____
Insurance	$_____
Pet Care	$_____
Subscriptions	$_____
Other:_____	$_____
TOTAL (B)	$_____

PERSONAL CARE EXPENSES:
Clothing	$_____
Toiletries	$_____
Barber/salon	$_____
Life Insurance	$_____
TOTAL (C)	$_____

CHILDCARE EXPENSES:
Tuition	$_____
Babysitting	$_____
Child support	$_____
Sports/Rec.	$_____
TOTAL (D)	$_____

SAVINGS:
Savings Account	$_____
Emergency fund	$_____
College savings	$_____
Investments	$_____
Retirement	$_____
Other:_____	$_____
TOTAL (E)	$_____

OBLIGATIONS:
Student loans	$_____
Taxes (Federal & State)	$_____
	$_____
Credit card	$_____
Credit card	$_____
Other:_____	$_____
TOTAL (F)	$_____

TRANSPORTATION EXPENSES:
Vehicle payment	$_____
Fuel	$_____
License/registration	$_____
Public transit	$_____
Insurance	$_____
Maintenance	$_____
Other: :_____	$_____
TOTAL (G)	$_____

HEALTHCARE EXPENSES:
Office visits	$_____
Prescriptions (Rx)	$_____
Health insurance	$_____
Gym membership/sports	$_____
Other:_____	$_____
TOTAL (H)	$_____

ENTERTAINMENT EXPENSES:
TOTAL (I)	$_____

CALCULATIONS

Total Gross Income:	$_____
Minus Total Expenses (A-I)	- $_____
= Equals	$_____
	(surplus/deficit)

Common Cent$

Living above your means can be a root issue to living paycheck to paycheck. Many people are discovering that non-essential expenses can be reduced or simply eliminated to bring their budgets into balance and their goals into focus.

Review your budget together. Can you locate areas in your budget where you can cut cost?

Expenses	Currently Spending	Possible Changes	A difference of...	Tips to help you Save
Utilities	$	$	$	_____ _____
Communication -Cell Phone -Home Phone -Internet -TV Service	$	$	$	_____ _____ _____ _____ _____
Food	$	$	$	_____ _____
Auto Expenses	$	$	$	_____ _____
Entertainment	$	$	$	_____ _____
Clothing	$	$	$	_____ _____
Insurance	$	$	$	_____ _____
Debt (credit cards, loans...)	$	$	$	_____ _____
Other_____	$	$	$	_____ _____
Other_____	$	$	$	_____ _____

UNDERSTANDING THE TITHE

OPPORTUNITY TO PROSPER!!!!!!

You may have noticed a category on the budget sheets that you have never seen before, *Opportunity for Prosperity*. As Believers, this section is not only a "must have" in your budget but a vital component to the design of a Christian's financial home. It is important to grasp the concept of kingdom increase through sowing financially into ministry soil to fund the Gospel. The Apostle Paul explains it like this:

> *"Remember: A stingy planter gets a stingy crop; a lavish planter gets a lavish crop. I want each of you to take plenty of time to think it over, and make up your own mind what you will give. That will protect you against sob stories and arm-twisting. God loves it when the giver delights in the giving. God can pour on the blessings in astonishing ways so that you're ready for anything and everything, more than just ready to do what needs to be done. As one Psalmist puts it,*
>
> > *He throws caution to the winds,*
> > *giving to the needy in reckless abandon.*
> > *His right-living, right-giving ways*
> > *never run out, never wear out.*
>
> *This most generous God who gives seed to the farmer that becomes bread for your meals is more than extravagant with you. He gives you something you can then give away, which grows into full-formed lives, robust in God, wealthy in every way, so that you can be generous in every way, producing with us great praise to God.*
>
> *Carrying out this social relief work involves far more than helping meet the bare needs of poor Christians. It also produces abundant and bountiful thanksgivings to God. This relief offering is a prod to live at your very best, showing your gratitude to God by being openly obedient to the plain meaning of the Message of Christ. You show your gratitude through your generous offerings to your needy brothers and sisters, and really toward everyone. Meanwhile, moved by the extravagance of God in your lives, they'll respond by praying for you in passionate intercession for whatever you need. Thank God for this gift, His gift. No language can praise it enough!"* **2Corinthians 9:6-16 (MSG)**

It's Only 10%

There are many opportunities for believers to sow financially into ministries: to feed the needy, pastor appreciation, offerings, various funds, etc. The greatest lack of understanding unfortunately lies in the area of the **TITHE (10%)**. As adults we would love to keep 90% of our pay each pay period but that is impossible. Our daily expenses and other financial obligations quickly consume it, which often leaves many living pay check to pay check. Isn't it great that God only ask us for just 10% while others pressure us for the rest and then some? According to a consumer expenditure survey gathered from the US Bureau of Labor Statistics, this is how the average family spends their income:

Category	% of Overall Spending
Housing (mortgage/rent, real estate taxes)	24%
Utilities(water/sewage, power and gas)	8%
Food	14%
Clothing	4%
Medical/Healthcare	6%
Donations/Gifts to Charity	**4%**
Savings and Insurance	9%
Entertainment and Recreation	5%
Transportation (car payment, gas, service)	14%
Personal/Debt Payments/Misc	12%

It's amazing how people have no problem paying the above mentioned expenses regardless of what percentage of their income is affected, yet many have concerns about sowing 10% of their income back into their home church. Please be aware that neither financing companies, utility companies, nor local stores truly concern themselves with where you spend eternity or the condition of your spirit man. Regardless of the percentage breakdown of your expenses, don't overextend yourself with financial obligations and neglect giving to your church.

As believers, we are not bound by a law or commandment to give but we are given the privilege to do so with great benefits. Tithing is an extension of who we are and how we honor God our Father.

What single thing would have to happen for you to feel that you are making financial progress over the next 12 months?

_____

_____

_____

Making Adjustments

Start with your goals in mind and then review your budget. You might find that you may need to establish priorities and adjust your budget to accomplish your goals. You see we serve a Mighty God who wants you to prosper financially. His grace of prosperity upon our lives and His principles of financial stewardship are the keys we need to properly manage our finances and reap the harvest that He has for His people. Having an attitude of gratitude and not a heart of covetousness and greed ushers us to a place that is pleasing to God. Our act of stewardship allows God to examine our hearts and ultimately determine our willingness to carry out His plans. Luke 16:10-12 **(KJV)** reads:

> *"He that is faithful in that which is least is faithful also in much: and he that*
> *is unjust in the least is unjust also in much.*
> *If therefore ye have not been faithful in the unrighteous mammon,*
> *who will commit to your trust the true riches?*
> *And if ye have not been faithful in that which is another man's,*
> *who shall give you that which is your own?"*

The key point here is faithfulness. What should be expected as a result of being an unfaithful steward?

_____

_____

_____

****************************BUILDING BLOCKS****************************

Romans 13:7 (NLT)
"Give to everyone what you owe them: Pay your taxes and government fees to those who collect them, and give respect and honor to those who are in authority."

Proverbs 6:1-3 (NLT)
"My child, if you have put up security for a friend's debt or agreed to guarantee the debt of a stranger—if you have trapped yourself by your agreement and are caught by what you said, follow my advice and save yourself, for you have placed yourself at your friend's mercy. Now swallow your pride; go and beg to have your name erased."

Proverbs 27:23 (CEB)
"Know your flock well; pay attention to your herds,"

I Thessalonians 5:12-13a (MSG)
"And now, friends, we ask you to honor those leaders who work so hard for you, who have been given the responsibility of urging and guiding you along in your obedience. Overwhelm them with appreciation and love!"

*********************SAY IT AND CREATE IT***********************

Confession:

"Father, we declare that we are good stewards over the finances that You have blessed us with. We thank You for the mustard seed of faith that You have given us in Your Word. Thank You Father for supplying all of our needs according to Your riches in glory by Christ Jesus (Phil 4:19) We identify ourselves as financial farmers looking for opportunities to sow into rich soil. We thank You for promising to give seed to the sower and using our family as a distribution center on behalf of Your kingdom. We understand how we handle our finances today will determine our financial destiny tomorrow. Father, we thank You for gracing us to recognize areas of overspending and teaching us how to live contently within our means. We proclaim that we will pass down a rich heritage of wealth management to our children, in Jesus name!

NOTES

_____
_____
_____
_____
_____
_____
_____
_____
_____
_____
_____
_____
_____
_____
_____
_____
_____
_____
_____

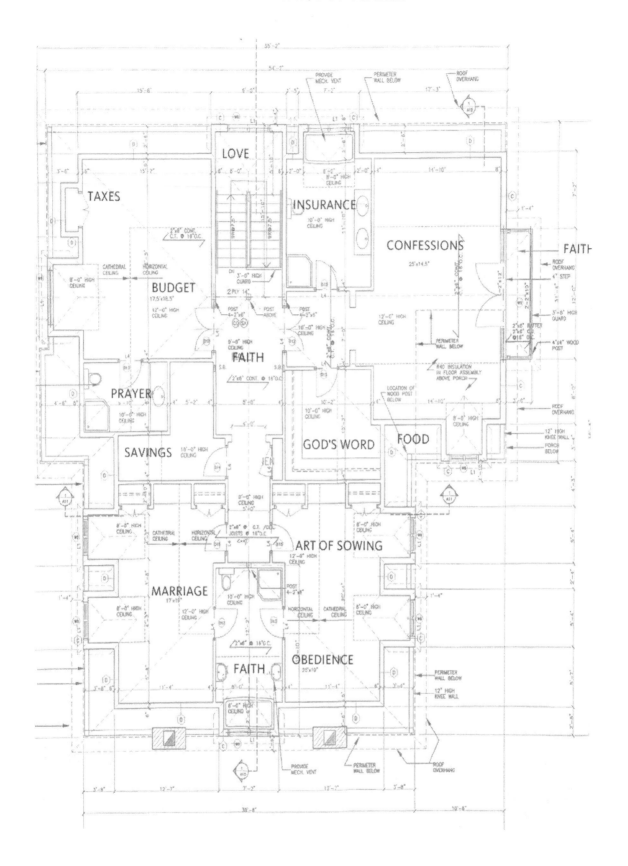

PHASE 5

CONSTRUCTING YOUR ROOF

Phase 5

Constructing Your Roof

Building Principle:

Plan with the future in mind.

Memory Verse:

> *"We can expect seventy years, or maybe eighty, if*
> *we are healthy, but even our best years bring trouble*
> *and sorrow. Suddenly our time is up and we disappear.*
> *Teach us to use wisely all the time we have."*
> **Psalms 90:10, 12 (CEV)**

Overview

Many people, if given the choice between money and time, will choose money. We have been taught the importance of money in our society; yet if spent, money is something that we can get (or earn) back. On the other hand, very little if any thing at all, is taught on the true value of time. Time wasted or spent can never be regained. That is why our memory verse encourages us to use our time wisely. The purpose of this phase is to encourage you to take time to cover you and your family. It is important to do it in a "timely" manner. "Life happens" and that's why it is so important to create a security plan to cover you against life's uncertainties.

Building Objectives:

- ➢ Understanding the importance of saving.
- ➢ Learning the benefits of having insurance.
- ➢ Knowing the benefits of preparing for the unexpected.
- ➢ Designing your retirement nest egg.
- ➢ Investment tips.

Understanding the Importance of Saving in Your Building Process

Our ability to save is such an important component of our roof. God is counting on us to be wise stewards. If the wealth we have is properly managed, we will be able to accomplish more for God's Kingdom on earth. When was the last time the Lord led you to give to someone in need, or give a love offering to your church? Or simply bless someone that you love? When was the last time that you were willing but felt unable to follow through with God's instructions to give? God wants to bless us so that we can be a blessing; however, being a blessing in a state of financial lack is often difficult and frustrating. Take a lesson from Paul as he confronted the Corinthian church on giving to those in need:

> *"On the first (day) of each week let each one of you [personally] put aside something and save it up as he has prospered [in proportion to what he is given], so that no collections will need to be taken after I come"*
> **I Corinthians 16:2 (AMP)**

It's unfortunate that many in the Body of Christ are living in a financial deficit. If they are not able to provide for their own basic needs, how can they provide for the needs of others? Lack is definitely not of God.

God is looking for those who are willing to assist with bringing in the harvest. He is interested in laborers that are willing to be distribution centers on behalf of His Kingdom. As a body, we have a lot of work to do. Each one has to help the other so that collectively we can accomplish more for the Kingdom of God. We can't accomplish much with insufficient funds.

The truth is we have to be wise stewards over our finances. We need to be mindful of our money management habits. Have faith in God. Know that God's Word works.

It is not enough for us to look wealthy. God wants us to *be* wealthy. As we begin to prosper God's way, we will not only appear wealthy but our lives will be fulfilled. Please take the truth and be set free, change your mind-set and discipline yourself to save. The Word says:

> *"Wise people live in wealth and luxury, but fools spend whatever they get it."* **Proverbs 21:20 (NLT)**

What teachings from your past shaped your beliefs on saving?

_____

_____

What do you feel are some obstacles that you may have regarding saving?

_____

_____

When you discipline yourself you will begin to see the importance of building your savings as well as the Kingdom of God.

Benefits of Saving

> ➤ It increases your ability to help others in need.
> ➤ You are able to prevent or reduce the need for credit.
> ➤ There is the possibility of avoiding consumer debt.
> ➤ It enhances your capability of spreading the gospel (a viable instrument for the Kingdom of God).

Benefits of Insurance

Planning for the unexpected is vital for the construction of your roof. Making plans to cover the ones you love offers you the peace of mind that your wishes will be carried out according to the Word of God and your moral beliefs.

There are believers who feel that the purchase of insurance shows lack of faith in God. According to them, this is unscriptural. Insurance is simply a means of safeguarding your family or someone else against unforeseen circumstances. God never promised in His word that believers would live a hazard free life. King Solomon taught:

> *"A prudent man sees danger and takes refuge,*
> *but the simple keep going and pay the penalty."* **Proverbs 2:3 (NIV)**

God encourages us in His word to take precautionary measures to avoid the unfavorable effects of the unforeseen.

We have taken the responsibility of properly covering our families with the following types of insurance: (check all that apply)

> ❑ Life Insurance
> ❑ Health Insurance
> ❑ Home/Renter's Insurance
> ❑ Automobile Insurance
> ❑ Disability Insurance
> ❑ Long Term Care Insurance
> ❑ Other _____
> ❑ Other _____

Benefits of Estate planning

As you begin this financial phase of building your financial home, you should take the time to consider how and to whom God would want you to transfer your wealth. It is also necessary to consider the guardianship of your children in the event of death.

"To every thing there is a season, and a time to every purpose under the heaven: A time to be born, and a time to die…" **Ecclesiastes 3:1-2 (KJV)**

It is a misconception that estate planning is only for the wealthy. Estate planning is however for those who desire to have a more orderly transfer of their assets upon death. It empowers you to make your own decisions while clarifying your intentions as to how you want your estate to be handled. Family relationships have been ruined as a result of lack of planning in this area. Imagine or think back to a homegoing service of a loved one. Family and friends should have loved and comforted one another instead they were feuding. This often happens as a result of trying to make decisions based on their own individual wishes as opposed to those of the deceased.

We serve a God of order and not a God of confusion. Take quality time to discuss topics such as these with those that you love and preserve your family's love and legacy forever.

Test your knowledge of key appointments involved in planning an estate:

_____ A signature by this person (or persons) is needed to certify the authenticity of a will (usually not a beneficiary).

_____ Alice, a widow with no kids passed away. She was very proactive before dying and assigned a dear responsible friend to pay off her debt, file her taxes, hire an attorney and distribute her remaining assets according to her wishes. Alice appointed _____.

_____ Ron laid out his desires for his brother Mark to manage his property upon his death . Ron knows that Mark values and love his nieces and will honor his wishes by maintaining his estate until they (Ron's daughters) reach maturity. Mark is Ron's _____.

_____ The Taylors sat down to discuss who they felt should care for their two sons in the event of them dying while their boys were young. They chose someone whose morals, values and religious beliefs line up with theirs. They are in the process of appointing _____.

_____ *"A good man leaveth behind an inheritance to his children and children's children."* (Proverbs 13:22) In other words, he/she will leave behind an inheritance to their _____.

_____ Josh and Morgan got married four months ago and they will be expecting their first child in seven months. A co-worker reminded Josh to visit their HR department to review his retirement plan and insurance policies. Josh needs to make a few adjustments and designate his new wife and unborn child as _____ so that his assets can go directly to them.

_____ Ms. Jones appointed her daughter Kim as _____ upon being diagnosed with Multiple Sclerosis. Kim will be responsible for making medical decisions for her mom if she becomes incapacitated.

Word Bank
A. Trustee
B. Heirs(s)
C. Health Proxy
D. Guardian
E. Witness
F. Beneficiary(ies)
G. Executor

Estate Planning Tips:

- ✓ Take inventory of your valued and cherished assets.
- ✓ Discuss important decisions with family members (or close friends).
- ✓ Periodically update your documents, especially after such events as:
    - Marriage
    - Birth of a child/grandchild
    - Death of a loved-one
    - Changing jobs
    - Divorce
    - As required by law (*research the laws in your state)
- ✓ Make a will and (or) establish a trust.

Designing Your Retirement Nest Egg

Many people reach retirement quicker than expected and, unfortunately, are unprepared.

Take some time to think about and write what your vision for retirement looks like. It doesn't matter if you're young and feel as if retirement is too far off to plan, or more mature and feel that it's too late to consider. Now is always a good age to start! Detailed notes can serve as a starting point for planning your retirement. Ask yourself questions like:

- ¤ At what age will I retire?
- ¤ Can I realistically afford to retire?
- ¤ What would be my housing arrangements?
- ¤ Is leisurely travel a part of my retirement plans?
- ¤ Do I plan to start another career or go back to school?
- ¤ Is volunteering and serving others a part of my retirement plans?

Our Plans for Retirement are…

_____
_____
_____
_____
_____
_____
_____
_____
_____
_____
_____
_____
_____
_____

Tips on Building a Great Investment Portfolio...

#1 – Invest from your <u>surplus</u> **(Matthew 14:20)**

#2 – Seek Godly wisdom **(Proverbs 15:22)**

#3 – Pray for discernment and carefully evaluate your risk **(Proverbs 14:15)**

#4 – Guard your heart from greed **(Luke 12:15)**

#5 – Know that it is God who gives you the power to get wealth **(Deuteronomy 8:18)**

#6 – Avoid the get rich quick attitude **(Proverbs 13:11)**

#7 – Diversify your investments **(Ecclesiastes 11:2)**

#8 – Sow Seeds **(Galatians 6:7)**

#9 – Invest in God's most precious commodity…YOU! **(Philippians 1:6)**

Self-Investment

Take time to invest in yourself. God's Word offers us such great inspiration and He has great plans for each of us. Paul says:

> *"Making mention of you in my prayers…That you may know what is the hope of His calling, what are the riches of the glory of His inheritance in the saints, and what is the exceeding greatness of His power toward us who believe.*
> **Ephesians 1:18-19 (NKJV)**

I once heard an awesome man of God use an illustration worth sharing. He said, "You will probably never find a person that will disregard the instructional manual of their automobile maker and go to their refrigerator with the intent of getting orange juice to fuel their vehicle." People highly regard their possessions so much that they are committed to looking over them and studying of their owner's manuals. Without a doubt, they rely on the product's maker to navigate them through the use of the product. If we can rely on human instructional manuals, how much more valuable is the greatest and most resourceful manual of all times, THE BIBLE. This is a more effective manual for life's challenges, our marriages, raising our children, dealing with our enemies, handling our finances and succeeding in life (to name a few).

Our Father has great plans in store for us. He wants us to have the courage to take the plans that He laid out in our hearts and minds and build it on His Word and faith in Him. Start taking time to learn what the Bible, our Manual of Life, has to say about you. And just like you're willing to protect your purchases by reading the user's guide, protect that which the Blood of our Savior, Jesus Christ purchased, and get the best out of this life that He paid the price for.

As Believers we should:

- ✓ Spend time daily studying God's Word.
- ✓ Be prayerful and allow Him to show us His purpose for our lives.
- ✓ Take time to research our heart's desires.
- ✓ Have a trusting heart and be willing to step out on faith believing God for His promises.

Many Believers are afraid to take risk; thereby missing God-given opportunities to usher them into a wealthy place. Chris Gardner, a homeless man turned millionaire, once said, "If you're not willing to take a risk on yourself, what will you take a risk on?"

What has God told you to do?

We are often complacent with where we are that we see no need for advancement. This is not supposed to be so. God wants to take us higher. God's financial plans for us are greater than what we can imagine. He wants to take us far beyond what we could imagine or think but we keep limiting Him. As the Body of Christ, we have great work to accomplish on earth. He has given us great potential, incredible dreams, creativity, wisdom and His supernatural power to broaden our horizon for the purpose of the Kingdom. Invest in the most important asset you have, YOURSELF, and stop letting the enemy tell you what you cannot do. Stop allowing the enemy to paralyze your building potential. Regardless of the size of your financial dream home, God's dream home for you far exceeds that. We have to take the gospel to those who are in bondage. We can't do it wishing we could, broke and in lack and we definitely can't do it in fear.

Take time and share your visions and dreams with your spouse (fiancé). It's virtually impossible for a Christian marriage to reach its fullest potential if the couple neglects to share each other's visions and dreams. If you fail to discuss your future, how can you move forward together? Jesus warns us in both Mark 3:25 and Luke 11:17 **(CEB)** that…
> *"…a house torn apart by division will collapse."*

What vision has God given you?

An online dictionary resource gave three good definitions of a vision.

1. The act or power of anticipating that which will or may come to be.
2. An experience in which a personage, thing or event appears vividly or credibly to the mind, although not actually present, often under the influence of a divine or other agency.
3. A vivid, imaginative conception or anticipation.

I define a vision as a God given idea, dream or revelation which when nurtured properly, will guide you towards your God given purpose.

God told the Prophet Jeremiah:

> *"Before I formed you in the womb I knew you; Before you*
> *were born I sanctified you;.."* **Jeremiah 1:5 (NKJV)**

God created us for His purpose. He knew us before we were formed in our mother's womb. He graced us with gifts and talents to fulfill the visions that He has given each of us.

The Problem:

➢ Many fail to spend quality time with Him and therefore fail to accomplish their vision.

➢ Others fail to develop a relationship with Him and therefore, never come to realize that there is a vision.

➢ Some walk in fear and never pursue their vision.

➢ Most give up, cave in and quit and never complete their vision.

➢ Then there are those who have their own agenda and are unable to clearly focus on the vision that God has given them.

What do you believe God has called you to do?

His:_____

Hers:_____

What obstacles do you think are in your way?

His:_____

Hers:_____

Have you shared your vision   His   Hers
with your spouse/fiancé?
                              ____   ____   ____   ____
                              Yes   **No**   **Yes**   **No**

"I can do all things through Christ which strengtheneth me."
Philippians 4:13 (NKJV)

Believing the above scripture, list ways to overcome obstacles that are trying to stop you from accomplishing the vision that God has given you for your life.

_____
_____
_____
_____
_____
_____
_____
_____

Write your vision

Habakkuk 2:2 tells us to

> *"... Write the vision, and make it plain upon tablets, that he may run that readeth it".*

What if you were told that your dreams and visions were God given and that your TRUE financial abundance was directly linked to that which God has inspired you to do? How would you handle them?

His:_____
_____
_____

Hers:_____
_____
_____

Use your vision pages to:

- ❏ Write your vision for your family down in details
- ❏ Ask God for guidance
- ❏ Use pictures and other illustrations as visual aides
- ❏ Explain how your vision will benefit the Kingdom of God
- ❏ Write scriptures and confessions for encouragement
- ❏ Pray with each other over your vision (or for a vision)
- ❏ Encourage and hold one another accountable as you work towards fulfilling it

VISION PAGE

VISION PAGE

*****************************BUILDING BLOCKS*****************************

Proverbs 22:3 (NCV)
"The wise see danger ahead and avoid it,
  but fools keep going and get into trouble."

2 Corinthians 12:14 (CEV)
"...Children are not supposed to save up for their parents, but parents are supposed to take care of their children."

1 Timothy 5:8 (CEV)
"People who don't take care of their relatives, and especially their own families, have given up their faith. They are worse than someone who doesn't have faith in the Lord."

Ecclesiastes 9:11 (MSG)
"...The race is not always to the swift, Nor the battle to the strong, Nor satisfaction to the wise, Nor riches to the smart, Nor grace to the learned. Sooner or later bad luck hits us all."

2 Timothy 1:6 (CEV)
"So I ask you to make full use of the gift that God gave you when I placed my hands on you. Use it well."

**************************SAY IT AND CREATE IT**************************

Confession: (write your personal faith confession over your family's vision)

_____

_____

_____

_____

_____

_____

_____

_____

_____

_____

_____

NOTES

_____

_____

_____

_____

_____

_____

_____

_____

_____

_____

_____

_____

_____

_____

_____

_____

_____

_____

_____

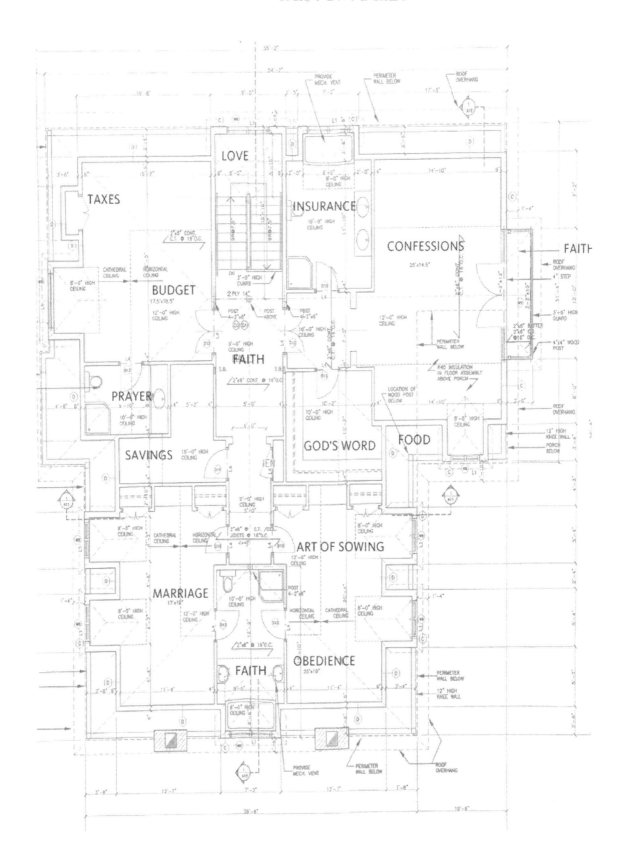

PHASE 6

HOME WARRANTY PLAN

Phase 6

Home Warranty Plan

Building Principle:

Be a good steward.

Memory Verse:

"Let them shout for joy, and be glad, that favour my righteous cause: yea, let them say continually, Let the Lord be magnified, which hath pleasure in the prosperity of His servant." **Psalm 35:27 (KJV)**

Overview

This is the most important phase of this book. It explains why trusting in God and His Word offers you the best protection for your *"Financial Home"*. God's home warranty plan [The Bible] offers you the ultimate peace of mind when it is understood and used for its intended purpose. He placed His plans for your finances in His Word to protect you and your family against financial setbacks. He teaches you how to maintain your financial home and the importance of doing so. Make sure that you fully understand His plan of prosperity by studying His Word and applying it to your finances.

Building Objectives:

➢ Trusting God with your finances.
➢ Understanding Seedtime and Harvest.
➢ Understand the purpose for your wealth.

"In God We Trust"

Now that you have complete instructions on how to build your financial home, protecting and maintaining it is vital.

People spend many years trying to figure out how to obtain financial success. Regardless of your financial status, I have learned that both the rich and the poor face challenges to some degree with regards to money management. Contrary to what many believe, one doesn't have to be poor to experience financial struggles. One who is wealthy is not necessarily financially secure. I pray for all of God's children to find peace in knowing that we simply need to trust in Him and believe in His Word.

> *"Trust in the Lord with all your heart. And lean not on your own understanding."* **Proverbs 3:5 (NIV)**

Why do you think that we would be encouraged to trust God and not our own understanding? The answer is found in His Word:

> *"For my thoughts are not your thoughts, neither are your ways my ways, saith the Lord."* **Isaiah 55:8 (KJV)**

Unfortunately, so many people constantly rely on their human perception and knowledge gathered from the world. Relying solely on our own ability and what we have been taught often yields results that are unfavorable. For example, if a person was brought up in an environment in which those around them argued and fought about household finances, typically that person has been conditioned to do the same. Imagine if that same person was taught and conditioned to go to the Word of God and/or pray over their finances they should expect different results.

You have to change your way of thinking to line up with His Word.

Do You Trust God?
> *"For the love of money is the root of all kinds of evil. And some people, craving money, have wandered from the true faith and pierced themselves with many sorrows."* **1 Timothy 6:10 (NLT)**

What does the Bible say about money?

It is so important that the Body of Christ have a clear understanding that money itself is not evil. There is absolutely nothing wrong with having money. God simply does not want money to have us. The wrong use of money has destroyed marriages, spoiled children, ruined relationships, and has brought unfruitfulness to the Kingdom. Money's true purpose has been over shadowed by greed, fear, covetousness and selfishness. This has hindered the spreading of the Gospel.

Below are a few spiritual issues that consume the mindsets of many people.

TENDENCIES	SPIRITUAL ISSUES	SPIRITUAL SOLUTION
1. Miser's mindset	A. Fear of lack	**T**
		R
2. Get rich quick	B. Lack of patience	**U**
		S
3. Overspending	C. Lack of contentment	**T**
4. Poverty mentality	D. Shortsightedness	**G**
		O
5. Envy	E. Covetousness	**D**

MATCH THE SPIRITUAL TENDENCIES WITH THE VERSES BELOW.

1.) *"He said to his disciples, 'Why are you so afraid? Do you still have no faith?'"* **Mark 4:40 (NIV)**   _____

2.) *"Wealth inherited quickly in the beginning will do you no good in the end."* **Proverbs 20:21 (NCV)**   _____

3.) *"Don't wear yourself out trying to get rich. Be wise enough to know when to quit."* **Proverbs 23:4 (NLT)**   _____

4.) *"Those who love money will never have enough. How meaningless to think that wealth brings true happiness!"* **Ecclesiastes 5:10 (NLT)**   _____

5.) *"The simple believes everything, but the prudent gives thought to his steps."* **Proverbs 14:15 (ESV)**   _____

6.) *"Then Jesus said to them, 'Be careful and guard against all kinds of greed. Life is not measured by how much one owns.'"* **Luke 12:15 (NCV)**   _____

7.) *"But I almost stumbled and fell, because it made me jealous to see proud and evil people and to watch them prosper."* **Psalms 73:2-3 (CEV)**   _____

MISER -   One who is reluctant to spend money even to the point of neglecting their personal needs. A **miser** typically has a goal of increasing or saving their money with no meaningful purpose. They compulsively hoard money out of greed, selfishness, or fear of lack.

How does trusting in God affect a **miser's** mindset about handling money?

_____

_____

_____

GET RICH QUICK - An urgency to build wealth quickly. A person might possibly have a desire to gain great wealth to escape their current financial situation, improve their lifestyle or impress others. They might not understand that God may be trying to develop them where they are currently or test and strengthen their faith in Him. One who has a desire to **get rich quick** often has a goal to gain great wealth using opportunities that are not thoroughly thought out.

How does trusting in God affect the desires of one who wants to **get rich quick**?

_____

_____

_____

OVERSPENDER - One who consistently spends over and above their financial means. An **over spender** is usually characterized by compulsively purchasing things that they want or desire, and often disregarding their needs and obligations. They typically spend out of fear of lack, greed, lack of contentment or lack of self-control.

How does trusting in God affect a person's tendencies to over spend?

_____

_____

_____

POVERTY MENTALITY- One who has a **poverty mentality** often view life with limits of little to no possible chances for improvement. They are often times complacent with lack and insufficiencies. They lack expectations of God's best of what life has to offer. This is not a Kingdom mindset. They are not knowledgeable of their covenant rights as children of the Most High God.

How does trusting in God affect one who has a **poverty mentality**?

_____

_____

_____

ONE WHO IS ENVIOUS OF OTHERS - is resentful of other people's achievements and desires (or covets) the good fortunes of others. They are use to murmuring and complaining. Their murmuring keeps them bound just as the Israelites who wandered in the wilderness for forty years because of their grumbling.

How does trusting in God alleviate a person's desire to "keep up with the Joneses"?

_____

_____

_____

Understanding the true purpose for acquiring Wealth

The true purpose for you prospering financially far exceed your own personal fulfillment, wants or desires. God wants us to recognize the fact that He created money with a purpose in mind. God wants us rich for the Kingdom. We are reminded in Proverbs 16:4 (**NLT**):

> *"The Lord has made everything for His own purpose."*

Does the purpose for your financial home line up with God's purpose?

God knows your wants and desires but that's not the main reason. He wants His children to prosper financially. He tells us in Matthew 6:33 (**KJV**)

> *"But seek ye first the kingdom of God, and his righteousness; and all these things shall be added unto you."*

God first wants our focus to be on the Kingdom while knowing and trusting that He in return will fulfill His covenant promises to us.

Consider this activity.

You are given $5,000 to spend in 5 minutes. Sounds easy? You might start to envision giving some to your church, paying on bills, stashing some away into various accounts and of course, treating yourself and some loved ones to a few things.

What if the money is entrusted to you with specific instructions?

> You cannot spend any of this money on yourself or for personal use (bills, debt, etc…)
> You must be a blessing to others
> You must keep an account of who you are blessing and why
> You cannot tell anyone but your spouse (fiancé)
> The two of you must be in agreement

We gave …	How much?	Because…	Who agree? His Hers
Example: * Miss Jane Doe	$ 500	She has always been a blessing to us and she's a great help with the kids	X X
* _____	$_____	_____	___ ___
* _____	$_____	_____	___ ___
* _____	$_____	_____	___ ___
* _____	$_____	_____	___ ___
* _____	$_____	_____	___ ___

Now consider...

> Your friends are planning a vacation getaway and invited the two of you. The total cost is $ 650.00 per couple. Until now you didn't have money to join them.
> Your car has been stalling and you have been thinking about getting a new one. A thousand plus your trade-in could be a nice down payment.
> A local electronics store is having a really good sale and you have been discussing how much you want a newer model TV or possibly another computer.
> You have not updated your wardrobe in years and could definitely do so now with all the good sales. Plus, now you have some extra money.
> Your anniversary is coming up and you would like to plan a little celebration with friends and family. Or you and your fiancé can now include a few extras for the wedding that you had to omit as a result of your budget.

How do you now feel about the decisions that you charted?

_____
_____
_____

Are both of you still in agreement?

_____

"Don't think only of your own good. Think of other Christians and what is best for them." **I Corinthians 10:24 (NLT)**

As you can see, it is very easy for a person's wants and desires to overshadow the needs of others. Sometimes God simply wants to use us as a channel to flow His blessings into the lives of others. Every circumstance in your own life may not be perfect but it is always better than someone else's. It is so important that we open up our hearts to hear from God and seek His will and purpose for the wealth that He has entrusted with us. Often times a believer will disregard God's instructions for giving and allow suggestions from the enemy to overshadow God's requests.

For example:

A good friend of yours lost her job several months ago. As she diligently looks for a new job, she stands on the Word of God and prays for a financial miracle.
God lays it upon your heart to minister to your friend financially but you are thinking about the plans you have for the money (new shoes, trips, birthday gifts, etc...).

The Bible notes:

"He who observes the wind [and waits for all conditions to be favorable] will not sow, and he who regards the clouds will not reap." **Ecclesiastes 11:4 (AMP)**

************************BUILDING BLOCKS************************

Deuteronomy 29:9 (NLT)
"Therefore, obey the terms of this covenant so that you will prosper in everything you do."

Proverbs 16:2 (NCV)
"You may believe you are doing right, but the Lord will judge your reasons."

Joshua 1:8 (KJV)
"This book of the law shall not depart out of thy mouth; but thou shalt meditate therein day and night, that thou mayest observe to do according to all that is written therein: for then thou shalt make thy way prosperous, and then thou shalt have good success."

Ephesians 5:5 (NCV)
"You can be sure of this: No one will have a place in the kingdom of Christ and of God who sins sexually, or does evil things, or is greedy. Anyone who is greedy is serving a false god."

Psalm 37:4 (NIV)
"Delight yourself in the LORD and he will give you the desires of your heart."

Proverbs 11:25 (NIV)
"A generous person will prosper; he who refreshes others will himself be refreshed."

Luke 12:15 (NIV)
"Then he said to them, Watch out! Be on your guard against all kinds of greed; a man's life does not consist in the abundance of his possessions."

***************************SAY IT & CREATE IT*************************

Confession: (finish writing your personal faith confession over your attitude towards money)

Father, we acknowledge You as our source according to 1 Timothy 6:17... It is God Almighty that provides us with all things richly to enjoy. We rebuke the fear of lack and insufficiency, greed and selfishness, or the desire to compare ourselves to others. We fill our thoughts with the promises of God's provision....

_____
_____
_____
_____
_____
_____
_____
_____
_____
_____
_____
_____
_____
_____

NOTES

_____
_____
_____
_____
_____
_____
_____
_____
_____
_____
_____
_____
_____
_____
_____
_____

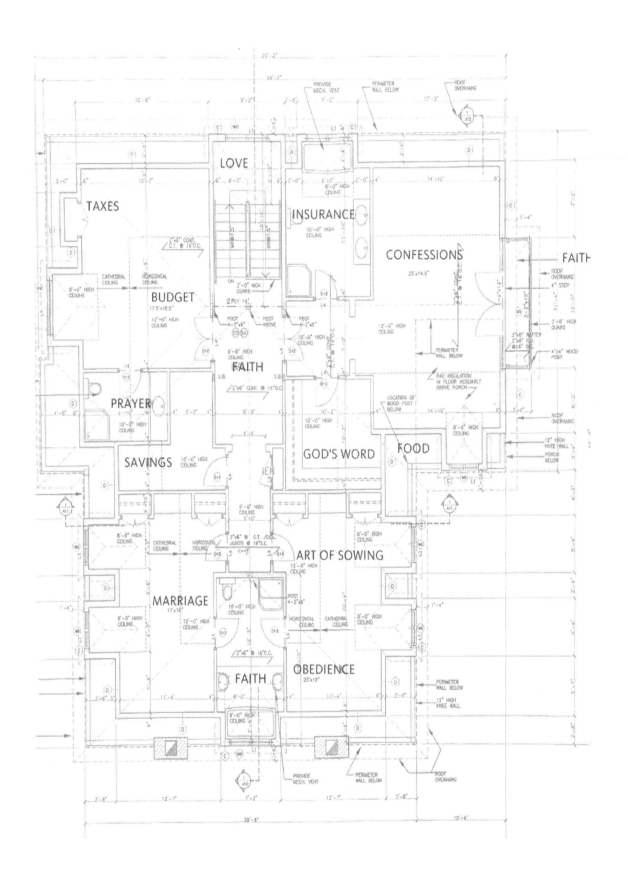

PHASE 7

SIGNING THE CONTRACT

Phase 7

Signing the Contract

Building Principle:

There is great power in agreement.

Memory Verse:

"Again, I tell you that if two of you on earth agree about anything you ask for, it will be done for you by my Father in heaven." **Matthew 18:19 (NIV)**

Overview

This phase is designed to seal the decisions that you have made to design and build your financial home based on stewardship principles that are in the Word of God. The Lord reminds us that His ways are not our ways. He guarantees us that His way of doing things will accomplish exactly what He intended. A fail proof guarantee to His promises is what the world's system can't offer or guarantee. Many believers have spent years handling their financial affairs outside of God's will and purpose for their lives. Financial prosperity is designed by God to manifest in our lives when we believe that He intended for us to have His best.

Building Objectives:

➢ Establish the basis for accountability.
➢ Serve as a reminder of your commitment.

Our Declaration of Faithful Financial Stewardship

From this day forward, we have decided to make a life a lifelong commitment of making financial choices according to God's Word. We make a decision to uphold God's principles of sound financial management and His grace of financial prosperity for us. After having realized that, our financial well-being is part of His will for our lives...

We agree to:

- Accept God's grace over our finances, believing that He has great plans to prosper us.
- Work as a team to fulfill God's ultimate purpose for our marriage and finances.
- Erase all fears of discussing money matters within our marriage.
- Be better stewards over the financial blessings that God has entrusted us with.
- Locate where we are financially and agree to live within our current means.
- Being committed to passing down a rich heritage of financial wisdom to our children and our children's children.
- Overcome financial obstacles and entrapments of the enemy.
- Trust God.
- _____

  Write your own

_____ & _____

Husband's Signature   _Wife's Signature_

_____

Date

_____

Witnessed By

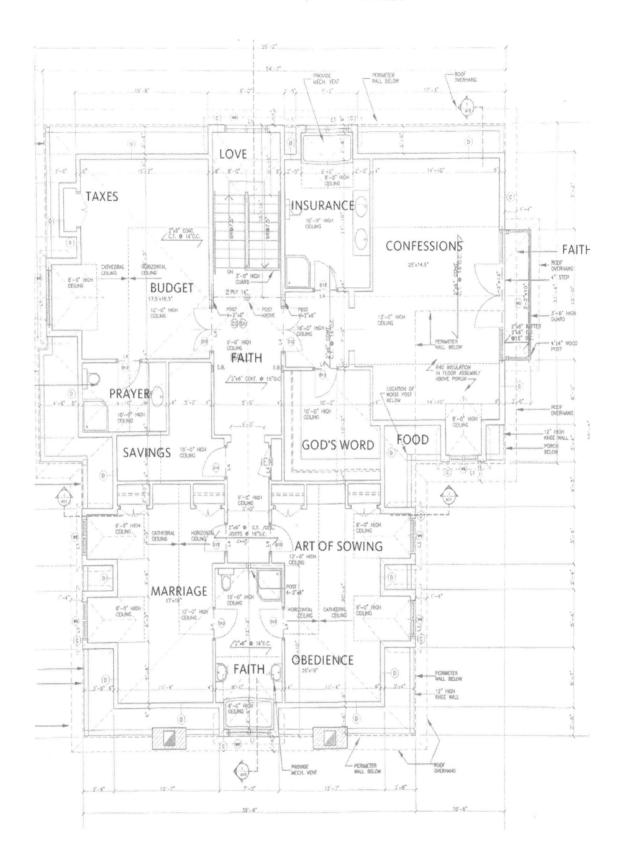

APPENDIX 1:
Final Walk-Through (Post-Test)

As of today, what is your first financial goal as a couple?

_____
_____
_____

What things made you afraid when you thought of surrendering your financial affairs to God?

_____
_____
_____

List some of the barriers that keep couples from working together in their finances?

_____
_____
_____
_____

What are the implications of a husband and wife not working together on their finances?

_____
_____
_____
_____

Are you communicating your financial plans effectively? _____
What areas are in need of improvements?

_____
_____
_____
_____

If couples knew that Satan was personally attacking them from accomplishing the ultimate will of God for their family, how would they act differently?

_____
_____
_____

What advice have you received about money in marriage that does not line up with God's Word?

_____
_____
_____
_____

How is working together as a couple for God's pleasure different from the way most people understand marriage?

_____
_____
_____
_____

What money management habits do non-believing couples have that should not be a part of a couple's financial plan?

_____
_____
_____
_____

How could you better manage your money?

_____
_____
_____
_____

"Wisdom is the principal thing; therefore get wisdom: and with all thy getting get understanding." **Proverbs 4:7 (KJV)**

This workbook does not have all the answers regarding how to manage your finances. What questions do you have in the different phases of your building process that you would like to learn more about?

☐ **Choosing Your Work Crew**

_____
_____
_____

☐ **Designing the Blueprints**

_____
_____
_____

☐ **Laying a Solid Foundation**

_____
_____
_____

☐ **Building Your Framework**

_____
_____
_____

☐ **Constructing Your Roof**

_____
_____
_____

☐ **Home Warranty Plan**

_____
_____

* Please be proactive in seeking the wisdom you need to make sound decisions that line up with God's Word.

APPENDIX 2:
Additional Work Sheets

INCOME AND EXPENSES

_____
Month & Year

GROSS INCOME:
    Salary $_____
    Salary $_____
    Child Support $_____
    Other:_____ $_____
    Other:_____ $_____
        TOTAL $_____

OPPORTUNITY TO PROSPER:
    Tithes $_____
    Offering $_____
        TOTAL (A) $_____

HOME EXPENSES:
    Mortgage/Rent $_____
    Electricity/Gas $_____
    Water/Trash $_____
    Phone/Internet $_____
    Cable/satellite $_____
    Groceries $_____
    Furnishings $_____
    Lawn care $_____
    Improvements $_____
    Cell Phones $_____
    Insurance $_____
    Pet Care $_____
    Subscriptions $_____
    Other:_____ $_____
        TOTAL (B) $_____

PERSONAL CARE EXPENSES:
    Clothing $_____
    Toiletries $_____
    Barber/salon $_____
    Life Insurance $_____
        TOTAL (C) $_____

CHILDCARE EXPENSES:
    Tuition $_____
    Babysitting $_____
    Child support $_____
    Sports/Rec. $_____
        TOTAL (D) $_____

SAVINGS:
    Savings Account $_____
    Emergency fund $_____
    College savings $_____
    Investments $_____
    Retirement $_____
    Other:_____ $_____
        TOTAL (E) $_____

OBLIGATIONS:
    Student loans $_____
    Taxes (Federal & State) $_____
        $_____
    Credit card $_____
    Credit card $_____
    Other:_____ $_____
        TOTAL (F) $_____

TRANSPORTATION EXPENSES:
    Vehicle payment $_____
    Fuel $_____
    License/registration $_____
    Public transit $_____
    Insurance $_____
    Maintenance $_____
    Other: :_____ $_____
        TOTAL (G) $_____

HEALTHCARE EXPENSES:
    Office visits $_____
    Prescriptions (Rx) $_____
    Health insurance $_____
    Gym membership/sports $_____
    Other:_____ $_____
        TOTAL (H) $_____

ENTERTAINMENT EXPENSES:
        TOTAL (I) $_____

CALCULATIONS

Total Gross Income: $_____

Minus Total Expenses (A-I) - $_____

= Equals $_____
        (surplus/deficit)

INCOME AND EXPENSES

_____
Month & Year

GROSS INCOME:
Salary $_____
Salary $_____
Child Support $_____
Other:_____ $_____
Other:_____ $_____
  TOTAL $_____

OPPORTUNITY TO PROSPER:
Tithes $_____
Offering $_____
  TOTAL (A) $_____

HOME EXPENSES:
Mortgage/Rent $_____
Electricity/Gas $_____
Water/Trash $_____
Phone/Internet $_____
Cable/satellite $_____
Groceries $_____
Furnishings $_____
Lawn care $_____
Improvements $_____
Cell Phones $_____
Insurance $_____
Pet Care $_____
Subscriptions $_____
Other:_____ $_____
  TOTAL (B) $_____

PERSONAL CARE EXPENSES:
Clothing $_____
Toiletries $_____
Barber/salon $_____
Life Insurance $_____
  TOTAL (C) $_____

CHILDCARE EXPENSES:
Tuition $_____
Babysitting $_____
Child support $_____
Sports/Rec. $_____
  TOTAL (D) $_____

SAVINGS:
Savings Account $_____
Emergency fund $_____
College savings $_____
Investments $_____
Retirement $_____
Other:_____ $_____
  TOTAL (E) $_____

OBLIGATIONS:
Student loans $_____
Taxes (Federal & State) $_____
  $_____
Credit card $_____
Credit card $_____
Other:_____ $_____
  TOTAL (F) $_____

TRANSPORTATION EXPENSES:
Vehicle payment $_____
Fuel $_____
License/registration $_____
Public transit $_____
Insurance $_____
Maintenance $_____
Other: :_____ $_____
  TOTAL (G) $_____

HEALTHCARE EXPENSES:
Office visits $_____
Prescriptions (Rx) $_____
Health insurance $_____
Gym membership/sports $_____
Other:_____ $_____
  TOTAL (H) $_____

ENTERTAINMENT EXPENSES:
  TOTAL (I) $_____

CALCULATIONS

Total Gross Income: $_____
Minus Total Expenses (A-I) - $_____
= Equals $_____
  (surplus/deficit)

_____ **INCOME AND EXPENSES**
Month & Year

GROSS INCOME:
Salary $_____
Salary $_____
Child Support $_____
Other:_____ $_____
Other:_____ $_____
      TOTAL $_____

OPPORTUNITY TO PROSPER:
Tithes $_____
Offering $_____
      TOTAL (A) $_____

HOME EXPENSES:
Mortgage/Rent $_____
Electricity/Gas $_____
Water/Trash $_____
Phone/Internet $_____
Cable/satellite $_____
Groceries $_____
Furnishings $_____
Lawn care $_____
Improvements $_____
Cell Phones $_____
Insurance $_____
Pet Care $_____
Subscriptions $_____
Other:_____ $_____
      TOTAL (B) $_____

PERSONAL CARE EXPENSES:
Clothing $_____
Toiletries $_____
Barber/salon $_____
Life Insurance $_____
      TOTAL (C) $_____

CHILDCARE EXPENSES:
Tuition $_____
Babysitting $_____
Child support $_____
Sports/Rec. $_____
      TOTAL (D) $_____

SAVINGS:
Savings Account $_____
Emergency fund $_____
College savings $_____
Investments $_____
Retirement $_____
Other:_____ $_____
      TOTAL (E) $_____

OBLIGATIONS:
Student loans $_____
Taxes (Federal & State) $_____
                             $_____
Credit card $_____
Credit card $_____
Other:_____ $_____
      TOTAL (F) $_____

TRANSPORTATION EXPENSES:
Vehicle payment $_____
Fuel $_____
License/registration $_____
Public transit $_____
Insurance $_____
Maintenance $_____
Other: :_____ $_____
      TOTAL (G) $_____

HEALTHCARE EXPENSES:
Office visits $_____
Prescriptions (Rx) $_____
Health insurance $_____
Gym membership/sports $_____
Other:_____ $_____
      TOTAL (H) $_____

ENTERTAINMENT EXPENSES:
      TOTAL (I) $_____

CALCULATIONS	
Total Gross Income:	$_____
Minus Total Expenses (A-I)	- $_____
= Equals	$_____
	(surplus/deficit)

INCOME AND EXPENSES

_____
Month & Year

GROSS INCOME:
Salary $_____
Salary $_____
Child Support $_____
Other:_____ $_____
Other:_____ $_____
          TOTAL $_____

OPPORTUNITY TO PROSPER:
Tithes $_____
Offering $_____
          TOTAL (A) $_____

HOME EXPENSES:
Mortgage/Rent $_____
Electricity/Gas $_____
Water/Trash $_____
Phone/Internet $_____
Cable/satellite $_____
Groceries $_____
Furnishings $_____
Lawn care $_____
Improvements $_____
Cell Phones $_____
Insurance $_____
Pet Care $_____
Subscriptions $_____
Other:_____ $_____
          TOTAL (B) $_____

PERSONAL CARE EXPENSES:
Clothing $_____
Toiletries $_____
Barber/salon $_____
Life Insurance $_____
          TOTAL (C) $_____

CHILDCARE EXPENSES:
Tuition $_____
Babysitting $_____
Child support $_____
Sports/Rec. $_____
          TOTAL (D) $_____

SAVINGS:
Savings Account $_____
Emergency fund $_____
College savings $_____
Investments $_____
Retirement $_____
Other:_____ $_____
          TOTAL (E) $_____

OBLIGATIONS:
Student loans $_____
Taxes (Federal & State) $_____
                                $_____
Credit card $_____
Credit card $_____
Other:_____ $_____
          TOTAL (F) $_____

TRANSPORTATION EXPENSES:
Vehicle payment $_____
Fuel $_____
License/registration $_____
Public transit $_____
Insurance $_____
Maintenance $_____
Other: :_____ $_____
          TOTAL (G) $_____

HEALTHCARE EXPENSES:
Office visits $_____
Prescriptions (Rx) $_____
Health insurance $_____
Gym membership/sports $_____
Other:_____ $_____
          TOTAL (H) $_____

ENTERTAINMENT EXPENSES:
          TOTAL (I) $_____

CALCULATIONS

Total Gross Income: $_____

Minus Total Expenses (A-I)   - $_____

= Equals $_____
                                (surplus/deficit)

INCOME AND EXPENSES

_____
Month & Year

GROSS INCOME:
Salary	$_____
Salary	$_____
Child Support	$_____
Other:_____	$_____
Other:_____	$_____
TOTAL	$_____

OPPORTUNITY TO PROSPER:
Tithes	$_____
Offering	$_____
TOTAL (A)	$_____

HOME EXPENSES:
Mortgage/Rent	$_____
Electricity/Gas	$_____
Water/Trash	$_____
Phone/Internet	$_____
Cable/satellite	$_____
Groceries	$_____
Furnishings	$_____
Lawn care	$_____
Improvements	$_____
Cell Phones	$_____
Insurance	$_____
Pet Care	$_____
Subscriptions	$_____
Other:_____	$_____
TOTAL (B)	$_____

PERSONAL CARE EXPENSES:
Clothing	$_____
Toiletries	$_____
Barber/salon	$_____
Life Insurance	$_____
TOTAL (C)	$_____

CHILDCARE EXPENSES:
Tuition	$_____
Babysitting	$_____
Child support	$_____
Sports/Rec.	$_____
TOTAL (D)	$_____

SAVINGS:
Savings Account	$_____
Emergency fund	$_____
College savings	$_____
Investments	$_____
Retirement	$_____
Other:_____	$_____
TOTAL (E)	$_____

OBLIGATIONS:
Student loans	$_____
Taxes (Federal & State)	$_____
	$_____
Credit card	$_____
Credit card	$_____
Other:_____	$_____
TOTAL (F)	$_____

TRANSPORTATION EXPENSES:
Vehicle payment	$_____
Fuel	$_____
License/registration	$_____
Public transit	$_____
Insurance	$_____
Maintenance	$_____
Other: :_____	$_____
TOTAL (G)	$_____

HEALTHCARE EXPENSES:
Office visits	$_____
Prescriptions (Rx)	$_____
Health insurance	$_____
Gym membership/sports	$_____
Other:_____	$_____
TOTAL (H)	$_____

ENTERTAINMENT EXPENSES:
TOTAL (I)	$_____

CALCULATIONS

Total Gross Income:	$_____
Minus Total Expenses (A-I)	- $_____
= Equals	$_____
	(surplus/deficit)

INCOME AND EXPENSES

_____
Month & Year

GROSS INCOME:
- Salary $_____
- Salary $_____
- Child Support $_____
- Other:_____ $_____
- Other:_____ $_____
- **TOTAL** $_____

OPPORTUNITY TO PROSPER:
- Tithes $_____
- Offering $_____
- **TOTAL (A)** $_____

HOME EXPENSES:
- Mortgage/Rent $_____
- Electricity/Gas $_____
- Water/Trash $_____
- Phone/Internet $_____
- Cable/satellite $_____
- Groceries $_____
- Furnishings $_____
- Lawn care $_____
- Improvements $_____
- Cell Phones $_____
- Insurance $_____
- Pet Care $_____
- Subscriptions $_____
- Other:_____ $_____
- **TOTAL (B)** $_____

PERSONAL CARE EXPENSES:
- Clothing $_____
- Toiletries $_____
- Barber/salon $_____
- Life Insurance $_____
- **TOTAL (C)** $_____

CHILDCARE EXPENSES:
- Tuition $_____
- Babysitting $_____
- Child support $_____
- Sports/Rec. $_____
- **TOTAL (D)** $_____

SAVINGS:
- Savings Account $_____
- Emergency fund $_____
- College savings $_____
- Investments $_____
- Retirement $_____
- Other:_____ $_____
- **TOTAL (E)** $_____

OBLIGATIONS:
- Student loans $_____
- Taxes (Federal & State) $_____
- $_____
- Credit card $_____
- Credit card $_____
- Other:_____ $_____
- **TOTAL (F)** $_____

TRANSPORTATION EXPENSES:
- Vehicle payment $_____
- Fuel $_____
- License/registration $_____
- Public transit $_____
- Insurance $_____
- Maintenance $_____
- Other: :_____ $_____
- **TOTAL (G)** $_____

HEALTHCARE EXPENSES:
- Office visits $_____
- Prescriptions (Rx) $_____
- Health insurance $_____
- Gym membership/sports $_____
- Other:_____ $_____
- **TOTAL (H)** $_____

ENTERTAINMENT EXPENSES:
- **TOTAL (I)** $_____

CALCULATIONS

Total Gross Income: $_____

Minus Total Expenses (A-I) - $_____

= Equals $_____
(surplus/deficit)

INCOME AND EXPENSES

_____
Month & Year

GROSS INCOME:
Salary $_____
Salary $_____
Child Support $_____
Other:_____ $_____
Other:_____ $_____
    TOTAL $_____

OPPORTUNITY TO PROSPER:
Tithes $_____
Offering $_____
    TOTAL (A) $_____

HOME EXPENSES:
Mortgage/Rent $_____
Electricity/Gas $_____
Water/Trash $_____
Phone/Internet $_____
Cable/satellite $_____
Groceries $_____
Furnishings $_____
Lawn care $_____
Improvements $_____
Cell Phones $_____
Insurance $_____
Pet Care $_____
Subscriptions $_____
Other:_____ $_____
    TOTAL (B) $_____

PERSONAL CARE EXPENSES:
Clothing $_____
Toiletries $_____
Barber/salon $_____
Life Insurance $_____
    TOTAL (C) $_____

CHILDCARE EXPENSES:
Tuition $_____
Babysitting $_____
Child support $_____
Sports/Rec. $_____
    TOTAL (D) $_____

SAVINGS:
Savings Account $_____
Emergency fund $_____
College savings $_____
Investments $_____
Retirement $_____
Other:_____ $_____
    TOTAL (E) $_____

OBLIGATIONS:
Student loans $_____
Taxes (Federal & State) $_____
     $_____
Credit card $_____
Credit card $_____
Other:_____ $_____
    TOTAL (F) $_____

TRANSPORTATION EXPENSES:
Vehicle payment $_____
Fuel $_____
License/registration $_____
Public transit $_____
Insurance $_____
Maintenance $_____
Other: :_____ $_____
    TOTAL (G) $_____

HEALTHCARE EXPENSES:
Office visits $_____
Prescriptions (Rx) $_____
Health insurance $_____
Gym membership/sports $_____
Other:_____ $_____
    TOTAL (H) $_____

ENTERTAINMENT EXPENSES:
    TOTAL (I) $_____

CALCULATIONS

Total Gross Income: $_____
Minus Total Expenses (A-I) - $_____
= Equals $_____
    (surplus/deficit)

INCOME AND EXPENSES

_____
Month & Year

GROSS INCOME:
Salary	$_____
Salary	$_____
Child Support	$_____
Other:_____	$_____
Other:_____	$_____
TOTAL	$_____

OPPORTUNITY TO PROSPER:
Tithes	$_____
Offering	$_____
TOTAL (A)	$_____

HOME EXPENSES:
Mortgage/Rent	$_____
Electricity/Gas	$_____
Water/Trash	$_____
Phone/Internet	$_____
Cable/satellite	$_____
Groceries	$_____
Furnishings	$_____
Lawn care	$_____
Improvements	$_____
Cell Phones	$_____
Insurance	$_____
Pet Care	$_____
Subscriptions	$_____
Other:_____	$_____
TOTAL (B)	$_____

PERSONAL CARE EXPENSES:
Clothing	$_____
Toiletries	$_____
Barber/salon	$_____
Life Insurance	$_____
TOTAL (C)	$_____

CHILDCARE EXPENSES:
Tuition	$_____
Babysitting	$_____
Child support	$_____
Sports/Rec.	$_____
TOTAL (D)	$_____

SAVINGS:
Savings Account	$_____
Emergency fund	$_____
College savings	$_____
Investments	$_____
Retirement	$_____
Other:_____	$_____
TOTAL (E)	$_____

OBLIGATIONS:
Student loans	$_____
Taxes (Federal & State)	$_____
	$_____
Credit card	$_____
Credit card	$_____
Other:_____	$_____
TOTAL (F)	$_____

TRANSPORTATION EXPENSES:
Vehicle payment	$_____
Fuel	$_____
License/registration	$_____
Public transit	$_____
Insurance	$_____
Maintenance	$_____
Other: :_____	$_____
TOTAL (G)	$_____

HEALTHCARE EXPENSES:
Office visits	$_____
Prescriptions (Rx)	$_____
Health insurance	$_____
Gym membership/sports	$_____
Other:_____	$_____
TOTAL (H)	$_____

ENTERTAINMENT EXPENSES:
TOTAL (I)	$_____

CALCULATIONS

Total Gross Income:	$_____
Minus Total Expenses (A-I)	- $_____
= Equals	$_____
	(surplus/deficit)

INCOME AND EXPENSES

_____
Month & Year

GROSS INCOME:
Salary $_____
Salary $_____
Child Support $_____
Other:_____ $_____
Other:_____ $_____
     TOTAL $_____

OPPORTUNITY TO PROSPER:
Tithes $_____
Offering $_____
     TOTAL (A) $_____

HOME EXPENSES:
Mortgage/Rent $_____
Electricity/Gas $_____
Water/Trash $_____
Phone/Internet $_____
Cable/satellite $_____
Groceries $_____
Furnishings $_____
Lawn care $_____
Improvements $_____
Cell Phones $_____
Insurance $_____
Pet Care $_____
Subscriptions $_____
Other:_____ $_____
     TOTAL (B) $_____

PERSONAL CARE EXPENSES:
Clothing $_____
Toiletries $_____
Barber/salon $_____
Life Insurance $_____
     TOTAL (C) $_____

CHILDCARE EXPENSES:
Tuition $_____
Babysitting $_____
Child support $_____
Sports/Rec. $_____
     TOTAL (D) $_____

SAVINGS:
Savings Account $_____
Emergency fund $_____
College savings $_____
Investments $_____
Retirement $_____
Other:_____ $_____
     TOTAL (E) $_____

OBLIGATIONS:
Student loans $_____
Taxes (Federal & State) $_____
                          $_____
Credit card $_____
Credit card $_____
Other:_____ $_____
     TOTAL (F) $_____

TRANSPORTATION EXPENSES:
Vehicle payment $_____
Fuel $_____
License/registration $_____
Public transit $_____
Insurance $_____
Maintenance $_____
Other: :_____ $_____
     TOTAL (G) $_____

HEALTHCARE EXPENSES:
Office visits $_____
Prescriptions (Rx) $_____
Health insurance $_____
Gym membership/sports $_____
Other:_____ $_____
     TOTAL (H) $_____

ENTERTAINMENT EXPENSES:
     TOTAL (I) $_____

CALCULATIONS

Total Gross Income: $_____

Minus Total Expenses (A-I) - $_____

= Equals $_____
            (surplus/deficit)

INCOME AND EXPENSES

_____
Month & Year

GROSS INCOME:
Salary $_____
Salary $_____
Child Support $_____
Other:_____ $_____
Other:_____ $_____
TOTAL $_____

OPPORTUNITY TO PROSPER:
Tithes $_____
Offering $_____
TOTAL (A) $_____

HOME EXPENSES:
Mortgage/Rent $_____
Electricity/Gas $_____
Water/Trash $_____
Phone/Internet $_____
Cable/satellite $_____
Groceries $_____
Furnishings $_____
Lawn care $_____
Improvements $_____
Cell Phones $_____
Insurance $_____
Pet Care $_____
Subscriptions $_____
Other:_____ $_____
TOTAL (B) $_____

PERSONAL CARE EXPENSES:
Clothing $_____
Toiletries $_____
Barber/salon $_____
Life Insurance $_____
TOTAL (C) $_____

CHILDCARE EXPENSES:
Tuition $_____
Babysitting $_____
Child support $_____
Sports/Rec. $_____
TOTAL (D) $_____

SAVINGS:
Savings Account $_____
Emergency fund $_____
College savings $_____
Investments $_____
Retirement $_____
Other:_____ $_____
TOTAL (E) $_____

OBLIGATIONS:
Student loans $_____
Taxes (Federal & State) $_____
$_____
Credit card $_____
Credit card $_____
Other:_____ $_____
TOTAL (F) $_____

TRANSPORTATION EXPENSES:
Vehicle payment $_____
Fuel $_____
License/registration $_____
Public transit $_____
Insurance $_____
Maintenance $_____
Other: :_____ $_____
TOTAL (G) $_____

HEALTHCARE EXPENSES:
Office visits $_____
Prescriptions (Rx) $_____
Health insurance $_____
Gym membership/sports $_____
Other:_____ $_____
TOTAL (H) $_____

ENTERTAINMENT EXPENSES:
TOTAL (I) $_____

CALCULATIONS
Total Gross Income: $_____
Minus Total Expenses (A-I) - $_____
= Equals $_____
(surplus/deficit)

INCOME AND EXPENSES

_____
Month & Year

GROSS INCOME:

Salary	$_____
Salary	$_____
Child Support	$_____
Other:_____	$_____
Other:_____	$_____
TOTAL	$_____

OPPORTUNITY TO PROSPER:

Tithes	$_____
Offering	$_____
TOTAL (A)	$_____

HOME EXPENSES:

Mortgage/Rent	$_____
Electricity/Gas	$_____
Water/Trash	$_____
Phone/Internet	$_____
Cable/satellite	$_____
Groceries	$_____
Furnishings	$_____
Lawn care	$_____
Improvements	$_____
Cell Phones	$_____
Insurance	$_____
Pet Care	$_____
Subscriptions	$_____
Other:_____	$_____
TOTAL (B)	$_____

PERSONAL CARE EXPENSES:

Clothing	$_____
Toiletries	$_____
Barber/salon	$_____
Life Insurance	$_____
TOTAL (C)	$_____

CHILDCARE EXPENSES:

Tuition	$_____
Babysitting	$_____
Child support	$_____
Sports/Rec.	$_____
TOTAL (D)	$_____

SAVINGS:

Savings Account	$_____
Emergency fund	$_____
College savings	$_____
Investments	$_____
Retirement	$_____
Other:_____	$_____
TOTAL (E)	$_____

OBLIGATIONS:

Student loans	$_____
Taxes (Federal & State)	$_____
	$_____
Credit card	$_____
Credit card	$_____
Other:_____	$_____
TOTAL (F)	$_____

TRANSPORTATION EXPENSES:

Vehicle payment	$_____
Fuel	$_____
License/registration	$_____
Public transit	$_____
Insurance	$_____
Maintenance	$_____
Other: :_____	$_____
TOTAL (G)	$_____

HEALTHCARE EXPENSES:

Office visits	$_____
Prescriptions (Rx)	$_____
Health insurance	$_____
Gym membership/sports	$_____
Other:_____	$_____
TOTAL (H)	$_____

ENTERTAINMENT EXPENSES:

TOTAL (I)	$_____

CALCULATIONS

Total Gross Income:	$_____
Minus Total Expenses (A-I)	- $_____
= Equals	$_____
	(surplus/deficit)

INCOME AND EXPENSES

_____
Month & Year

GROSS INCOME:
Salary $_____
Salary $_____
Child Support $_____
Other:_____ $_____
Other:_____ $_____
    TOTAL $_____

OPPORTUNITY TO PROSPER:
Tithes $_____
Offering $_____
    TOTAL (A) $_____

HOME EXPENSES:
Mortgage/Rent $_____
Electricity/Gas $_____
Water/Trash $_____
Phone/Internet $_____
Cable/satellite $_____
Groceries $_____
Furnishings $_____
Lawn care $_____
Improvements $_____
Cell Phones $_____
Insurance $_____
Pet Care $_____
Subscriptions $_____
Other:_____ $_____
    TOTAL (B) $_____

PERSONAL CARE EXPENSES:
Clothing $_____
Toiletries $_____
Barber/salon $_____
Life Insurance $_____
    TOTAL (C) $_____

CHILDCARE EXPENSES:
Tuition $_____
Babysitting $_____
Child support $_____
Sports/Rec. $_____
    TOTAL (D) $_____

SAVINGS:
Savings Account $_____
Emergency fund $_____
College savings $_____
Investments $_____
Retirement $_____
Other:_____ $_____
    TOTAL (E) $_____

OBLIGATIONS:
Student loans $_____
Taxes (Federal & State) $_____
     $_____
Credit card $_____
Credit card $_____
Other:_____ $_____
    TOTAL (F) $_____

TRANSPORTATION EXPENSES:
Vehicle payment $_____
Fuel $_____
License/registration $_____
Public transit $_____
Insurance $_____
Maintenance $_____
Other: :_____ $_____
    TOTAL (G) $_____

HEALTHCARE EXPENSES:
Office visits $_____
Prescriptions (Rx) $_____
Health insurance $_____
Gym membership/sports $_____
Other:_____ $_____
    TOTAL (H) $_____

ENTERTAINMENT EXPENSES:
    TOTAL (I) $_____

CALCULATIONS

Total Gross Income: $_____

Minus Total Expenses (A-I) - $_____

= Equals $_____
    (surplus/deficit)

Weekly spending plans allow you to better control your money and achieve your financial objectives.   Most people often feel as if they have more month than money and by the end of the month, they are robbing Peter to pay Paul. A weekly spending plan can help you prioritize your spending and make managing your money more achievable.

Weekly Spending Plan

_____
(Month & Year)

Income	$	$	$	$

Expenses	Week 1	Week 2	Week 3	Week 4
Totals	$	$	$	$

Weekly Spending Plan

(Month & Year)

Income	$	$	$	$

Expenses	Week 1	Week 2	Week 3	Week 4
Totals	$	$	$	$

Weekly Spending Plan

(Month & Year)

Income	$	$	$	$

Expenses	Week 1	Week 2	Week 3	Week 4
Totals	$	$	$	$

Weekly Spending Plan

(Month & Year)

Income	$	$	$	$

Expenses	Week 1	Week 2	Week 3	Week 4
Totals	$	$	$	$

Wealth Assessment Worksheet

ASSETS (what you own)

Cash:

Cash _____
Checking Acct. _____
Savings Acct. _____
Money Market _____
Cash Value of
    Life Insurance _____
Other: _____

Personal Property:

Personal Residence _____
Vacation Home _____
Automobiles _____
Collectibles _____
Jewelry/Furs _____
Recreational
    Vehicle(s) _____

Investments:

Certificates of Deposits _____
Mutual Funds _____
401(k), 403(b)… _____
Pension Plans _____
Stocks _____
Bonds _____
Annuities _____

Business:
Fair Market Value _____
Real Estate Value _____

Other:

_____ _____

LIABILITIES (what you owe)

Personal Loans:

Family/Friends _____
Educational _____
Financial Institutions _____

     _____
Life Insurance _____

Mortgage Loan _____
Vacation Mortgage _____
Automobile Loan _____
Other: _____
Other: _____

Current Debts:

Medical _____
Credit Card(s) _____
Department Store _____
IRS _____
Other: _____
Other: _____

Business Liability _____

_____ _____

Calculations: Date_____

Assets $_____
Liabilities (minus) -$_____
TOTAL: $_____

Wealth Assessment Worksheet

ASSETS (what you own)

Cash:

Cash   _____
Checking Acct.   _____
Savings Acct.   _____
Money Market   _____
Cash Value of
    Life Insurance   _____
Other: _____

Personal Property:

Personal Residence   _____
Vacation Home   _____
Automobiles   _____
Collectibles   _____
Jewelry/Furs   _____
Recreational
    Vehicle(s)   _____

Investments:

Certificates of Deposits   _____
Mutual Funds   _____
401(k), 403(b)…   _____
Pension Plans   _____
Stocks   _____
Bonds   _____
Annuities   _____

Business:
Fair Market Value   _____
Real Estate Value   _____

Other:

_____   _____

LIABILITIES (what you owe)

Personal Loans:

Family/Friends   _____
Educational   _____
Financial Institutions   _____

Life Insurance   _____

Mortgage Loan   _____
Vacation Mortgage   _____
Automobile Loan   _____
Other: _____
Other: _____

Current Debts:

Medical   _____
Credit Card(s)   _____
Department Store   _____
IRS   _____
Other: _____
Other: _____

Business Liability   _____

_____   _____

Calculations: Date_____

Assets $_____
Liabilities (minus) -$_____
TOTAL: $_____

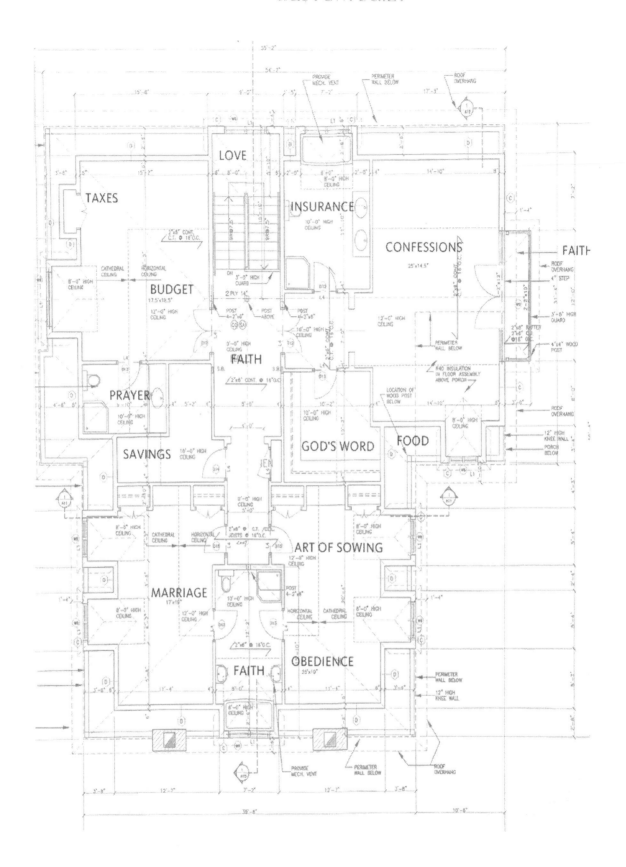

<u>APPENDIX 3:</u>
Credits

- Clason, George S. The Richest Man in Babylon. New York, NY: Penguin, 1955.

- "Vision." www.dictionary.com, LLC.Copyright © 2012 All rights reserved.

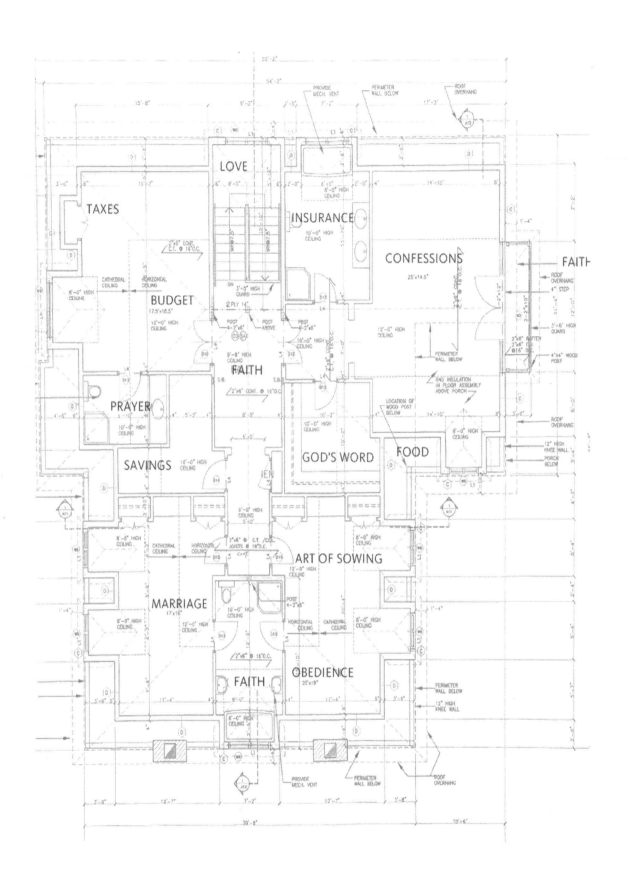

APPENDIX 4:
Answer Keys

Answer Keys

Building Verses

_____"The wicked borrows and does never repay..."
        Psalm 37:21 (NLT)   C

_____"Trust in the Lord with all thine heart: and lean
        not unto thine own understanding." **Proverbs 3:5(KJV)**   D

_____"If you have not been faithful in the use of that
        which is another's, who will give you that which
        is your own?" **Luke 16:12 (KJV)**   G

_____"The rich rules over the poor, and the borrower
        is servant to the lender." **Proverbs 22:7 (KJV)**   E

_____"Dishonest money dwindles away, but he who
        gathers money little by little makes it grow.
        Proverbs 13:11 (NIV)   H

_____"Two are better than one because they have a
        good [more satisfying] return for their labor."
        Ecclesiastes 4:9 (AMP)   B

_____"It is not wise to promise to pay what your
        neighbor owes." **Proverbs 17:18 (NCV)**   A

_____"But this I say, He which soweth sparingly shall
        reap also sparingly; and he which soweth bountifully
        shall reap also bountifully."
        2 Corinthians 9:6 (KJV)   F

Test your knowledge of key appointments involved in planning an estate: (pg. 66)

_____A signature by this person (or persons) is needed to certify
        the authenticity of a will (usually not a beneficiary).   E

_____Alice, a widow with no kids passed away. She was very   G
        proactive before dying and assigned a dear responsible
        friend to pay off her debt, file her taxes, hire an attorney
        and distribute her remaining assets according to her wishes.
        Alice appointed _____.

_____Ron laid out his desires for his brother Mark to manage his property   A
        upon his death. Ron knows that Mark values and love his
        nieces and will honor his wishes by maintaining his estate until they
        (Ron's daughters) reach maturity. Mark is Ron's _____.

Answer Keys

Test your knowledge of key appointments involved in planning an estate: (pg. 66) (con't)

_____The Taylors sat down to discuss who they felt should care for their two sons in the event of them dying while their boys were young. They chose someone who's morals, value and religious beliefs line up with theirs. They are in the process of appointing _____.   **D**

_____"A good man leaveth behind an inheritance to his children and children's children" (Proverbs 13:22). In other words, he/she will leave behind an inheritance to their _____.   **B**

_____Josh and Morgan got married four months ago and they will be expecting their first child in seven months. A co-worker reminded Josh to visit their HR department to review his retirement plan and insurance policies. Josh needs to make a few adjustments and designate his new wife and would be baby as _____ so that his assets can go directly to them.   **F**

_____Ms. Jones appointed her daughter Kim as _____ upon being diagnosed with Multiple Sclerosis. Kim will be responsible for making medical decisions for her mom if she becomes incapacitated.   **C**

Match the spiritual tendencies with the verses below. (pg 81)

_1.)_ "He said to his disciples, "why are you so afraid? Do you still have no faith?" **Mark 4:40 (NIV)**   1, 2, 4 & 5

_2.)_ "Wealth inherited quickly in the beginning will do you no good in the end." **Proverbs 20:21 (NCV)**   2

_3.)_ "Don't wear yourself out trying to get rich. Be wise enough to know when to quit." **Proverbs 23:4 (NLT)**   2

_4.)_ "Those who love money will never have enough. How meaningless to think that wealth brings true happiness!" **Ecclesiastes 5:10 (NLT)**   1, 2, 3 & 5

_5.)_ "The simple believes everything, but the prudent gives thought to his steps." **Proverbs 14:15 (ESV)**   2 & 4

_6.)_ "Then Jesus said to them, "Be careful and guard against all kinds of greed. Life is not measured by how much one owns." **Luke 12:15 (NCV)**   2, 3 & 5

_7.)_ "But I almost stumbled and fell, because it made me jealous to see proud and evil people and to watch them prosper." **Psalms 73:2-3 (CEV)**   5

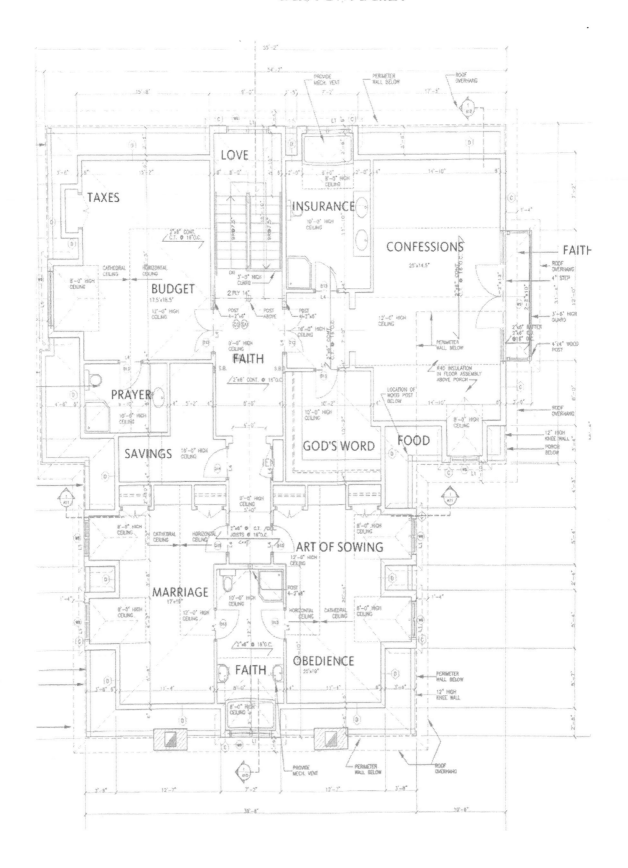

60332523R00075

Made in the USA
Lexington, KY
03 February 2017